As one of the world's longest establish
and best-known travel bran
Thomas Cook are the experts in trav

For more than 135 years o
guidebooks have unlocked the secre
of destinations around the worl
sharing with travellers a wealth
experience and a passion for travel.

**Rely on Thomas Cook as your
travelling companion on your next trip
and benefit from our unique heritage.**

Thomas Cook **traveller** guides

GOA
Anil Mulchandani

1873

Written by Anil Mulchandani, updated by Debbie Stowe

Published by Thomas Cook Publishing
A division of Thomas Cook Tour Operations Limited.
Company registration no. 3772199 England
The Thomas Cook Business Park, Unit 9, Coningsby Road,
Peterborough PE3 8SB, United Kingdom
E-mail: books@thomascook.com, Tel: + 44 (0) 1733 416477
www.thomascookpublishing.com

Produced by Cambridge Publishing Management Limited
Burr Elm Court, Main Street, Caldecote CB23 7NU

ISBN: 978-1-84848-240-1

© 2006, 2008 Thomas Cook Publishing
This third edition © 2010
Text © Thomas Cook Publishing
Maps © Thomas Cook Publishing/PCGraphics (UK) Limited
The international boundaries on maps are neither purported to be correct
nor authenticated by the Survey of India

Series Editor: Adam Royal
Production/DTP: Steven Collins

Printed and bound in Italy by Printer Trento

Cover photography: Reinhard Schmid, 4Corners Images

Contents

Introduction

India's smallest state, Goa presents visitors with most of the fascinating aspects of India in a microcosm. Although it is the sun-kissed beaches fringed with palms and lush tropical vegetation that draw travellers to Goa, an increasing number of visitors are travelling inland to see historic towns, medieval churches, mosques and Hindu temples, villages and their weekly markets, spice and Ayurvedic plantations, bird-filled lakes, wildlife sanctuaries, waterfalls and tribal hamlets in the hills of the Western Ghats.

The secular mix of people in India can best be experienced in the region generally referred to as Central Goa, between the Mandovi and Zuari rivers, including the state capital of Panaji which has Portuguese buildings, old quarters and cosmopolitan residential areas. Panaji is a short drive from the churches of Velha Goa or Old Goa, the former capital that is now a World Heritage Site, the medieval mosque of Ponda, and typically Goan temples where visitors can bear witness to Hindu religious rituals.

The coast is the first call for most visitors, and a huge travellers' scene has developed north of the Mandovi River at beaches like Calangute, Candolim and Baga, with thatched beach shacks, restaurants, cafés, hotels, watersports and recreational facilities. The scene is more 'alternative' further north at Anjuna and Vagator, and becomes less touristy towards Querem.

The beaches south of the Zuari River are known for their sophisticated infrastructure of luxurious resorts, five-star hotels and spas offering access to some of Goa's most attractive beaches. These luxurious accommodation facilities are also the base from which to explore the affluent towns and villages of South Goa with their grand old houses and imposing churches. The beaches further south, like Palolem, have a more low-key and laid-back atmosphere with palm-thatched huts and eateries.

Travelling inland from the coast, the hills of Goa have prehistoric finds, ancient Jain and Buddhist sites, and the gem of a temple at Tambdi Surla that is a fine example of the 13th-century architecture that thrived during the reign of the Vijayanagar Dynasty. For more examples of medieval Indian architecture, visitors to Goa travel into Karnataka to see the impressive remains of the citadel of Hampi and the temple complexes in and around Badami, while Bijapur has one of the finest collections of Islamic architecture in India.

In contrast to the laid-back charm of Goa's beaches and towns, and the medieval monuments of Karnataka, Mumbai (formerly Bombay) is India's busiest city and has one of the most crowded metros in the subcontinent. The international gateway to Goa for most travellers, Mumbai does, however, offer opportunities to escape the congested areas to explore ancient cave sites and colonial buildings. Mumbai is the capital of Maharashtra, the state that has hill stations like Mahableshwar – popular hill resort getaways from Goa for long-staying visitors – and princely towns like Kolhapur that are worth a stopover to see the palaces, eclectic buildings and nearby hill forts.

Yet more than the holiday at the beaches and the tours of the historic places, most visitors to Goa remember the smiling, charming, friendly and fun-loving Goan people who love their food and enjoy a good party.

Introduction

India

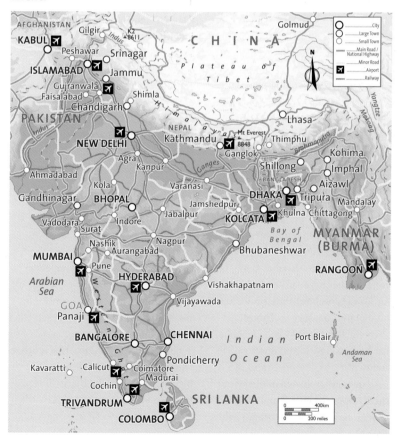

The land

The former Portuguese enclave of Goa occupies a narrow strip of land between the Arabian Sea and the Western Ghats. It owes much of its fame to the coastline that forms the western boundary of the state. Besides beach tourism, which is an important source of revenue for the state, parts of the coast, called khazans, have also been developed for shipping, fisheries and salt production.

Geography

Goa is India's smallest state, about 100km (62 miles) from north to south along the coast, and rarely exceeding 60km (37 miles) from west to east, where it shares common borders with Maharashtra to its north and northeast and Karnataka to its east and south. A number of rivers flow through the state, from Tiracol in the north to Galgibaga in the south, with the Mandovi and Zuari estuaries separating the two districts of North and South Goa. The estuaries are lined with mangrove forests that support a variety of birds and marine life.

Rising from the coast and along the rivers are the laterite plateaux that jut out seawards as headlands, providing the sites for forts such as Tiracol, Chapora, Aguada and Cabo De Rama that protected Goa from invaders. The laterite plateaux comprise most of Goa's densely populated midlands where terraced orchards and plantations grow spices, coconut palms and fruits such as pineapple, jackfruit, guava, papaya, banana and mango, with water flowing down to irrigate paddy fields and other lowland cultivation closer to the coast.

In the east are the Sahyadri ranges of the Western Ghats where the peaks exceed 1,100m (3,609ft) high. These hilly areas are among Goa's least populated and most thickly forested areas. The forests are inhabited by a variety of wildlife, including sloth bear, panther and gaur, and are a paradise for birdwatchers.

Economy

Goa is one of India's most prosperous states, with the highest per-capita income in the country, its economy boosted by remittances from Goans working in other states of India and overseas.

One of the biggest earners is tourism, which started in the 1960s when hippies discovered the charm of Goa's beaches. The tourism boom grew when charter flights brought in plane-loads of travellers. Since then, tourism has thrived in Goa, attracting high-spending foreign and Indian travellers to its five-star and boutique hotels, beach resorts and heritage hotels.

Although it has now been eclipsed by tourism, agriculture has traditionally been the foundation of the economy. The main food and cash crops are rice, maize, oilseeds, sugar cane, cashew nuts, spices, rubber, fruits, vegetables and garden plants. Goa also has a sizeable number of people reliant on fishing for their livelihood.

There are a number of small and medium-sized industrial units, especially those that make use of the state's natural resources, such as food processing and canning units. Iron ore and other minerals are major exports of Goa, and mining continues despite opposition from the environmental lobby.

Today, the government is encouraging investment and infrastructure development in other sectors, with a particular focus on information technology.

The land

Goa

History

321–184 BC Goa is part of the Kuntala administrative area under the Maurya Dynasty, the major power in India.

2nd century AD The Bhoj Dynasty rules from Chandrapur, near the present village of Chandor.

6th–10th centuries The Chalukyas of Badami rule Goa with the local Kadambas as their feudatories.

11th century The Kadambas build the new port of Goppakapatna or Govepuri (Gove). Trade with Zanzibar and Sri Lanka flourishes and ties are strengthened with Arab traders.

14th century Islamic invasions disrupt Goa. Gove is destroyed and Muhamad Tuglaq's army levels Chandrapur. The Muslims of the Deccan form the Bahmani Dynasty and take control of Goa. In 1378 the Hindu Vijayanagar Dynasty emerges victorious over the Bahmani Dynasty and Goa becomes part of their kingdom headquartered at Hampi. Trade thrives under the Vijayanagar Dynasty, especially the export of spices and the import of Arabian horses.

1469 The Bahmanis, under Muhamad Shah, capture Goa. They destroy the old capital of Govepuri and establish a new city, Gove, now known as Old Goa.

1489 The Bahmanis divide into factions. Yusuf Adil Shah, who established the Bijapur Sultanate, inherits Goa. He makes Gove his second capital and establishes a fort on the River Mandovi in the area that is now Panaji. Trade flourishes and Goa becomes an embarkation point for pilgrimages to Mecca.

1510 Portuguese Alfonso de Albuquerque attacks Goa and takes it successfully from Yusuf Adil Shah but loses it again a few months later. He attacks Goa again and takes it on St Catherine's day, 25 November. He massacres Muslims who had supported the sultan and gives powers to Hindus.

1542 St Francis Xavier arrives in Goa.

1560	The Inquisition ushers in a period of dissent. Hindus and Muslims alike are attacked in the areas of the 'Old Conquest'. Hindus are forbidden from practising their religion and even Christians live in fear.
17th century	The Dutch attack Goa and take Cochin. The Marathas attack Goa later in the century but move back following the threat of Mughal attacks on their territory.
1737–9	The Marathas attack Goa and take parts of North and South Goa. Settlement is reached between the Portuguese and the Marathas.
1781–91	The Portuguese make new conquests in Goa.
1787	The Pinto Revolt takes place, in which Goan churchmen ask for equal rights.
1797	The British occupy Goa, and the British garrison remains until 1813, despite Portuguese protests.
1812	Inquisition is abolished
1821	Goa is allocated representation in Lisbon's Parliament.
1843	Panaji is officially declared the capital of Goa.
1881	The first ever railway links are established between Mormugao and the peninsula of India.
1928	The Goa Congress Committee is formed.
1947	India becomes independent from British rule.
19 Dec 1961	The Indian national government, under Prime Minister Jawaharlal Nehru, opposes Portuguese rule over Goa. In December 1961, the Indian army mounts Operation Vijay and the Indian government designates Goa a Union Territory.
1987	Goa receives statehood.
1990s– 2005	Goa suffers from political instability, with 14 governments in 15 years.
2008	After a period of relative stability the state is hit by another political crisis when the Congress-led coalition government narrowly avoids collapse.
2011	National Games of India to be held in Goa.

Politics

A land of considerable religious diversity, India has sustained a constitutional democratic system, based on secularism, equal rights for women, universal suffrage, human rights and a ban on untouchability, for over 60 years, despite tremendous pressure and challenges. There were, however, two years when prime minister Indira Gandhi imposed a ban on political activity as an emergency measure.

Government of India

India is a sovereign democratic republic, and all citizens over 18 years of age are eligible to vote. The president is the official head, but exercises his or her powers under the authority of the prime minister and with the advice of the council of ministers who are selected by the prime minister.

There are two houses of parliament. The lower house, *Lok Sabha* or house of the people, comprises members elected by the constituencies of the country and two nominated members of the Anglo-Indian community. Of the 543 elected seats of the *Lok Sabha*, a significant minority are reserved for scheduled tribes and undereducated classes. The upper house, *Rajya Sabha* or council of states, has 12 members nominated by the president from a maximum of 250, with the rest elected by the state assemblies.

The 28 states and one self-governing union territory have legislative assemblies with the governor as the official head, nominated by the president, and a chief minister. The governor is responsible for the actual administration of the state with the cabinet of ministers. Like the central government, most of the states have two houses of parliament – the *Rajya Sabha* comprising mainly nominated members and the *Vidhan Sabha* consisting of the elected members.

There is a clear line of distinction between the role of central and state governments. The central government controls the armed forces, aviation, railways, postal services, currency and international affairs. The state governments are responsible for industry, agriculture, roads, forestry and environment, and internal security.

The political scene in India

The Indian National Congress Party has been a dominant force in the politics of India since 1885 when it was established as the first Indian national political institution. Jawaharlal Nehru became the first prime minister of India in 1947, and Congress won seven of the first ten general elections held in India. At the 11th general elections in 1996, Congress was defeated by the Bharatiya Janta Party (BJP). A coalition was formed, called the United Front, but it fell in 1998 when Congress withdrew support and the BJP came to power with Atal Behari Vajpayee as the prime minister. BJP won the elections in 1999 and Vajpayee once more became prime minister of India, but Congress scored a surprise victory in the 2004 elections and Manmohan Singh became prime minister. He was returned to office in 2009. In 2007, India's first female president, Pratibha Patil, was elected.

Goan government and politics

Goa was a union territory administered by the president of India until 1987 when it was given full statehood. It has a 40-member legislative assembly, with two seats in the *Lok Sabha* and one in the *Rajya Sabha*.

Congress won most of the elections in Goa in the 1980s and 1990s, but regional issues, such as the role of *Marathi* as a language, and the environment, are still key. President's Rule has been imposed on Goa several times since it achieved statehood, a reflection of Goa's political instability. In 2000, BJP took over the state administration, with Manohar Parriker as the chief minister. In 2005, Congress returned to power and Digambar Kamat was appointed chief minister in June 2007.

The old methods of tilling fields are still practised

Culture

In spite of 451 years of Portuguese rule, Goa retains most of its earlier cultural traditions. The Portuguese may have introduced Christianity to Goa, but even the local Catholic population follows a caste system similar to that of the Hindus. Christians, Hindus and Muslims recognise and participate in each other's religious festivals, and this contributes to Goa's relaxed atmosphere.

Caste

The Hindus follow a caste system that has to some extent spread to other religions. The four main castes are *Brahmin* (the priestly caste), *Kshatriya* (the warrior caste), *Vaishya* (the trading community) and *Sudra* (the agricultural caste). These castes are hereditary and have no relation to the occupation or financial status of the person today. The Saraswat, Padhya, Bhatt, Kramavant and Chitpavans are among the priestly group of *Brahmins*, while artisans like goldsmiths are called *Panchala Brahmins*.

Indigenous communities

The Kharvi Catholics claim to be the original inhabitants of Goa's coastal stretch. Descendants of Hindu fishing communities, they have accepted Portuguese names like Dias and D'Souza. The Thovois are Christian carpenters who provide furniture and woodcarvings to the churches of Goa.

The Kunbis, Velips, Gowada and Dhangars are among the oldest communities of Goa; while many of them have joined the mainstream, some Kunbis and Velips still live in traditional thatch-roofed houses, herding livestock on the southern hillsides and following ancestral worship rituals. Traditionally, Kunbi women wear copper bangles on their arms, bead necklaces, and oiled hair tied into distinctive coils. The Lambanis from Karnataka visit Goa to sell their wares at Mapusa Market and Anjuna Flea Market.

Music and dance

Goans are known in India and abroad for their love of music and dance. With their long exposure to European influences, Goan musicians are in great demand for westernised music and dance performances that are the rage in India today.

The most typical dance of Goa is the *mando*, a Konkani love song accompanied by a stringed instrument like the violin and a percussive instrument like the local terracotta drum. The men and women dance in two rows, the men carrying colourful hankies and the women sporting fans. Other dances of Goa are the Portuguese-style *corridinho*, martial dances such as *ghode modni*, Hindu *dhalo* and *fugdi* dances, the harvest dance called *gof*, and the percussive stick dance called *tonyamel*. Local street plays, called *tiatr*, are usually performed in the Konkani language.

Language

The official language of Goa is Konkani, written in the Devanagri script, and it has been the medium of instruction at schools since 1991. Marathi is also widely spoken and taught. Only a few Goans still consider Portuguese their second language, but English is now a popular medium of instruction. The national language, Hindi, is taught as a second language in school.

Women in traditional dress at Anjuna Market

Religion

With its many churches and its colonial history, Goa gives first-time visitors the impression that it is a Christian majority state, but in fact the majority of Goans follow Hinduism. Christians are the largest minority, and there is a small population of Muslims, while Parsees, Jains and Sikhs have migrated to Goa attracted by the income opportunities offered by tourism here. Though ancient Buddhist sites have been found in Goa, most of the Buddhists in the state today are migrants from Nepal and Tibet.

Hinduism

Hinduism is a religious tradition with ancient roots dating back to the third and second millennia BC. With no founder, prophet or church-like organisation to define the rules, Hinduism has embraced new features and a diversity of religious beliefs even until recent times. The holy books of the Hindus are the *Vedas* (incorporating the *Upanishads* as the final volumes), which are often considered the foundation of Indian philosophy, with epics like the *Ramayana* and *Mahabharata*, and the *Bhagavad Gita* which is based on the philosophies of Lord Krishna as they were related to warrior prince Arjun in an episode of the *Mahabharata*.

Hindus believe in a cycle of reincarnation determined by their *karma*, the consequences of former actions that can flow into the next life. The aims of a Hindu are to attain material wealth honestly (*artha*), satisfy all desires (*kama*) and perform all duties (*dharma*), all of which will lead, through good *karma*, to *moksha*, liberation from the endless rebirth cycle.

An aspect of Hinduism that most visitors to India find hard to understand is the multitude of gods and goddesses. Actually, most of them are incarnations and manifestations of a few, and this may be the result of Hinduism incorporating regional beliefs into its pantheon. Three Gods are considered integral to Hinduism: Brahma as the creator, Vishnu as the preserver of the universe (usually worshipped as one of his many incarnations that rid the world of destroying forces like demons) and Shiva, the destroyer, who is worshipped in many forms, such as Natraja when he dances to destroy evil. The consort of Brahma is Sarasvati, the goddess of learning. Vishnu's consort Lakshmi is worshipped as the goddess of wealth, and Shiva's consort Parvati has many manifestations, including Durga and Kali, goddesses of power and destruction. Most Hindus start a new venture by worshipping Ganesh, the elephant-headed son of Lord Shiva, who is said to bring luck, knowledge and prosperity.

Some key features of Hindu religious traditions are *darshan* ('to see'), which denotes the importance of visiting holy places, *puja* or ritualistic worship, and cremation of the dead.

An interesting Hindu tradition in Goa is the reverence of the basil plant (*tulsi*) that is grown outside temples and most Goan Hindu houses.

Christianity

The Portuguese introduced Roman Catholicism to Goa soon after their arrival in 1510. Since then, most Goan Christians belong to the Roman Catholic Church, one of the world's largest Christian groups tracing descent from the Western Catholic Church. They acknowledge the authority of the Pope, whose utterances are considered binding.

Pope Clement VII erected the See of Goa on 31 January 1533, with a wide-ranging jurisdiction. St Francis Xavier, a Jesuit, arrived here in 1542 and administered to the Goan Christians. The Jesuits established the first printing press in India and published their works in vernacular languages.

In 1557, Goa was made an Archbishopric, with suffragans (assistant bishops) in other parts of India. In 1572, Pope Gregory XIII, in his *Brief*, dated 15 March, acknowledged the Archbishop of Goa as the Primate of the East. Since 1928, this Archdiocese has been known as 'Goa and Daman'.

The Portuguese instigated harsh policies to impose Catholic orthodoxy on the people of Goa. A tribunal called the Goa Inquisition was set up in 1560: Hinduism was banned and Christians lived in fear. The Inquisition met regularly and held great public trials, with execution of those they believed were infidels. Punishment ranged from stripping the victims of their possessions or detaining them in

Hindu shrines are dedicated to particular deities and are important places of *puja* – ritualistic worship

dungeons to public strangling and even burning at the stake. Later centuries saw the suppression of religious orders, with the Jesuits banned in 1759.

Islam

Islam began in Mecca around the 7th century, when the Prophet Muhammad compiled revelations from Allah. The *Quran* is the holy book of the Muslims and the supreme authority on the Islamic faith. The five pillars of Islam are the profession of faith regarding the one God and Muhammad as God's messenger (*shahada*), worshipping five times daily, almsgiving, fasting in the month of *Ramadhan*, and the pilgrimage to Mecca. Alcohol and pork are prohibited and meat must be prepared in a way called *halal* that involves draining the blood of an animal while it is alive. Gambling and charging interest on loans are forbidden.

Buddhism

Buddhism is based on the beliefs of Sidhartha Gautama Buddha who was born into a princely family in the 6th century BC. His preaching is often regarded as a reaction to Hinduism, accepting the doctrine of reincarnation and the law of *karma*, but rejecting the concept of a pantheon of gods and the caste system.

The Buddha preached that there are noble truths: life is painful, suffering is the result of past *karma*, ignorance and desire, and that beyond this suffering is *nirvana*, which can be achieved by following an eight-fold path of right knowledge, right attitude, right speech, right action, right living and occupation, right effort, right discipline and right composure.

Jainism

Like the Buddhists, the Jains in Goa are immigrants from other states like Gujarat and Rajasthan, although the forests of Bicholim and Satari are said to have been refuges of Jains and Buddhists from resurgent Hinduism and Islamic invasions. There are a few Jain temples in Goa, most of them recent.

Jainism was founded by Vardhaman or Mahavir, whom Jains revere as the 24th *tirthankar* (ford-makers, as these prophets or saints are said to create bridges across the rivers of life through their philosophies). He left his noble home and became an ascetic, achieving enlightenment after 12 years of penance and meditation. Much of the Jain art seen at museums and in the temples (*derasars*) is based on the tales of the 24 *tirthankars*.

The key features of the Jain religion are liberation from the wheel of rebirth and the belief that all life is sacred. Strict vegetarianism is a feature of Jainism, for Jains believe that even the smallest life form has a soul.

The virtues in Jainism are *ahimsa*, which is non-violence (non-harming of any living thing); honesty; speaking the truth; chastity; and non-attachment to

Statue of Buddha, Ambedkar Garden, Panaji

Religion

Interior of St Catejan Church, Old Goa (*see p48*)

worldly possessions. Intentional injury is seen as the worst sin.

Zoroastrianism

The Zoroastrians came to India in the 8th century, landing on the Gujarat coast from the Persian Gulf, and are known as Parsees. Parsees trace their belief back to Zoroaster, an Iranian prophet of the 6th or 7th century BC, and their holy book is the *Avesta*.

Zoroastrians believe in one god, Ahura Mazda, seen as rejecting evil for good and purifying thought, word and action. The focal point for Zoroastrian worship is the fire from ancient times, and earth and air are also considered sacred.

Sikhism

Sikhism was founded by Guru Nanak who was born in Punjab in the 15th century. Guru Nanak accepted the idea of a cycle of rebirths and karma, or the result of previous action, from Hinduism, but believed that there is just one god who is formless, eternal and omnipresent, and he opposed the caste system. Guru Nanak preached the importance of *naam* (meditating and prayer on God's name), *Daan* (charity) and *snana* (bathing) to achieve harmony. At the core of the religion is the idea of the 'guru'. Sikhs believe that God is the true guru, and that the path to salvation is found through regarding him as the centre for he is merciful. God's word came to humankind through ten people called gurus, from Guru Nanak to Guru Gobind Singh, each chosen by their predecessor on the basis of his spiritual insight into God.

It was Guru Gobind Singh who gave Sikhism the features that make a Sikh recognisable from any other Indian. He introduced the Khalsa brotherhood, which required a Sikh to have uncut hair called *kesh*, carry a comb or *kanga*, usually made from wood, own a *kirpan*, which is a dagger or sword, sport a *kara* or steel bangle, and wear a *kach* or shorts, reflecting military tradition because this new community was to be powerful in both defending the religion and in establishing a moral society. This community was strictly opposed to discrimination on the basis of caste or sex, and the last name of Singh given to males, and Kaur, or princess, given to females ensured that there were no names indicating caste, and indicated that women had an equal standing with men.

The devout Sikh begins each day with meditative worship and recitation of Guru Nanak's worship. The congregational worship encouraged by Guru Amar Das, the third guru, takes place in *gurudwaras* that come under a central controlling authority. Guru Amar Das also established the communal kitchen tradition, or *langar*, to encourage all castes to eat together without prejudice. This *langar*, paid for by the *gurudwara*, serves as a way to remove caste prejudice, to strengthen a feeling of community and to help the underprivileged.

Festivals

Most Hindu, Christian and Muslim festivals are well observed in Goa, with the intermingling of religious communities being a special feature of the ceremonies. Hindu and Muslim festivals follow the lunar calendar, which differs from the western calendar, and dates can be checked with the tourist offices in Goa. The state also has a growing number of arts and cultural events.

Feast of the Three Kings

6 January

This festival is celebrated with re-enactments of the three kings bringing gifts for Jesus Christ. The best places to witness the celebrations are Chandor, Cansaulim and Reis Magos where a large fair is held at the 16th-century church.

Mahashivratri

February/March

This is a Hindu festival commemorating the night when Lord Shiva danced the *tandav*, the dance of destruction, with ceremonies at Arvelam, Fatorpa, Mangesh, Nangesh, Queula and Shiroda temples.

Carnival

February/March

Celebrating the arrival of spring, the Carnival takes place shortly before the start of Lent. A non-religious event, it is a good time to see Goans in full celebratory mode. The event is opened by a Goan appointed as the life of the party and playing the part of King Momo (King of Misrule), who makes a decree ordering his 'subjects' to forget their worries and have a good time. On *Sabado Gordo* (Fat Saturday), he leads a colourful procession of floats through the streets, with depictions of Goan folk culture and contemporary messages, musicians, people dancing the *mando* and competing teams in flamboyant costumes. Carnival is one big party, the revelry lasting for three days, with dance parties at clubs and hotels.

Shigmotsav

March

Shigmo marks the climax of spring, with pageants of fanciful floats and musicians playing percussive instruments. People have fun throwing coloured paint and water at each other. The festivities are best witnessed at Panaji, Margao, Vasco da Gama and Mapusa.

The Procession of All Saints
March

On the Monday of Holy Week each year there is a procession of floats featuring life-size statues of saints from St Andrew's Church at Goa Velha. The procession takes a loop from the church through the Goa Velha village and ends at the church square for a candlelit service. The saints' statues can be viewed for two days after the procession. This is the only procession of its kind outside Rome, and the tradition dates to the 17th century. The local fair offers good opportunities to buy handicrafts.

Feast of Our Lady of Miracles
March/April

Held 16 days after Easter, this festival is celebrated by Hindus and Christians, who gather to venerate the image of Nossa Senhora de Milagres and celebrate the feast day of the Sabin, on which a huge fair and market are held at Mapusa.

Ganesh Chaturthi
August/September

Lord Ganesh is venerated during this festival, which is one of the most popular Hindu events in Goa. On the last day of the festivities, the idols of Ganesh are paraded in a procession, accompanied by loud music, before immersion in the sea or at one of the rivers or inland lakes.

Christmas
25 December

As elsewhere, Christmas in Goa is the day for family gatherings, feasting and celebrations, and special sweets are prepared. The midnight Mass at Goa is called 'Cock Crow' because it traditionally goes on until the early hours of the morning.

Enjoying the colourful festival of Shigmotsav

Architecture

As a legacy of its unusual colonial history, Goa's architecture incorporates local and international influences. While the churches are Indian versions of European architecture, the temples integrate Muslim and European architecture into a traditional Hindu layout.

Churches

Churches are a dominant feature of Goa's landscape. They are usually positioned on hilltops or in the main squares of villages and towns. Generally constructed in European style, Goa's churches are distinguished by the rich heritage of Indian craftsmanship, which is evident even in the Church of Our Lady of Rosary, the oldest surviving church in Goa. The churches are often cruciform in construction, with a sanctuary comprising the main altar and a richly ornamented backdrop called the reredos, a chancel with murals or woodcarvings, side altars and a long hall for the congregation. They are usually whitewashed to protect the laterite walls, and they have deep-set windows that are suited to Goa's climate.

Italian Renaissance and Baroque influences are evident in those churches built between 1550 and 1650, when the Portuguese undertook church-building activities with a missionary zeal. This period saw the building of two of Goa's best-known monuments, the Se Cathedral and the Basilica of Bom Jesus. Some of the churches, such as St Cajetan Church of Old Goa, were entirely modelled on those of Rome.

The next hundred years saw the growth of the distinctive synthesis of Indian and Baroque architecture in churches like the Church of St Francis of Assisi in Margao (Madgaon), Santana in Talaulim, and the churches of Divar Island. The artisans were given more freedom and decorated the churches with Indian motifs.

In the churches of the 18th century, rococo features were incorporated into the design, and Indian artisans excelled in decorating the reredos, pulpits and vaulting of the chancels.

Goan houses

In the 18th and 19th centuries, Goa's wealthy families commissioned houses in keeping with their wealth and status. Built like other Konkani houses, with laterite walls, Mangalore red-tiled roofs and inner courtyards, these houses were purpose-built to entertain guests, with an attractive reception hall and rooms for the balls and banquets that were a feature of the Goan lifestyle. The concept of functional rooms, such as libraries and studies, was introduced in the new houses, while large Baroque and rococo windows, balconies and verandas kept the interior cool. Taking advantage of trade ties, the owners imported marble and mosaic tiles, mirrors and glass from Europe, and porcelain and china from Macao. The Goan carpenters created beautiful rosewood and teak furniture for these houses, taking inspiration from imported pieces and designs.

Temples

Goa has a number of Hindu temples, built during the 18th and 19th centuries, that have incorporated Christian and Muslim elements into traditional Hindu temple layouts of the porch, entrance hall, *mandapa* (hall) and *sanctum* (sanctuary). The *shikaras* (pyramidal towers with a bell-shaped section at the top), which are a feature of Hindu temples elsewhere, have been replaced in Goa by domes, *minarets* (slender towers with balconies) and East Indian roofs inspired by Mughal architecture. A unique feature of Goa's temples is the *deepasthamba*, or lamp tower, that looks like a column of light on festive occasions when lamps are lit in the niches of the towering structure.

A typical Goan temple tower

Impressions

A popular tourist destination for many years, Goa is geared up for travellers and offers a variety of modern facilities not easily available in other states of India. A compact state by Indian standards, travellers find it easy to tour the beaches, towns and villages even during a short stay. The state capital, Panaji, is small enough for a visitor to walk around and see the main sights of the town.

Getting around
Bus
Buses connect most towns and villages, and they are an economical and convenient way of getting around Goa, but they are often crowded and are not as comfortable as taxis. The state-owned Kadamba transport service has bus stations in the towns and stops at most villages. Ask at the bus station whether you need to buy tickets at the counter before getting on the bus or in the bus itself.

Private operators have attractive buses with comfortable seating to attract passengers, but often play loud music or videos. Most of these private buses connect Goa with Maharashtra and Karnataka.

Cars and taxis
Taxis are available at taxi stands in the main towns, outside popular hotels and resorts, at Dabolim Airport, Margao Railway Station, most bus terminals and near tourist places.

Make sure you fix the price before setting off.

An alternative is to hire a car with a driver from a tour operator, hotel travel desk or the Goa Tourism Development Corporation (GTDC). It is a good idea to hire a car for two or three days, which means you will be able to explore most of Goa's sights. The majority of drivers can speak English and act as interpreters, removing most of the usual hurdles that travellers face in India, such as asking for directions or accessing information. They also help to interact with locals and the government offices. The rental is either based on the number of hours with a kilometre allowance, or negotiated. If you hire a car for more than a day, the night halt charge includes the driver's expenses, and he will expect a tip at the end of the tour.

Self-drive car hire is still in its infancy in India, although a few companies, such as Hertz, Budget and Sai, do offer this service in Goa.

Cycling

Bicycles can be hired in most cities and towns of Goa. Indian cycles are heavy and do not have gears, but they are perfectly adequate for the flat coastal roads of Goa, and some operators now offer imported mountain bikes for hire. On the roadsides you will find repair shops that are nominally priced. Check the tyres and general condition of the cycle, and whether the bell and lights work. It may be a good idea to bring a light with you and a cord to strap down your baggage, as these are not easily available in India. Those travelling with children may find it necessary to bring a basket along or have one made. Do not leave your rucksack or any other baggage on the bicycle, as it could be an invitation to thieves.

If you bring your own bicycle with you, carry plenty of spares and a repair kit.

St Cajetan Church in Old Goa (*see p48*)

Ferries

Although bridges have been built across the rivers of Goa, and services are becoming fewer, flat-bottomed ferries still operate to islands like Divar or across to places like Tiracol Fort in the far north of the state. The ferries are usually crowded

Locals disembark from a Goan river ferry

with people, motor-cycles, scooters and cars.

Motorcycling

Motorbikes – ranging from 100cc to 350cc, and a few 500cc – can easily be hired in Goa. An alternative is the scooter, usually 100cc to 150cc, which has a lockable compartment for small items and a spare tyre on the back. Smaller mechanised bikes – mopeds – have no gears and are only suitable for short-distance travel.

It is a good idea to check the condition of the motorbike or scooter, and the documents (third-party insurance is compulsory in India), before hiring. An international driving licence is advisable.

Bring helmets with you, otherwise it may be necessary to buy them in Goa. Most travellers hiring motorbikes bring their own gloves, leathers, boots and other protective material. You can also ask the hotel travel desk for information about motorbike tour operators in Goa. Joining a tour can eliminate some of the hassles of hiring a motorbike and travelling in India.

Goa also has 'motorbike taxis' that are cheaper and faster than cars, but some insurance companies are known not to cover travellers for accidents on these.

Rickshaws

Auto-rickshaws are noisy and uncomfortable three-wheel vehicles with a driver in front and a bench or seats for two or more passengers. They are more economical than taxis and convenient for crowded and narrow streets because of their smaller size. They are also a fun, quintessentially Indian experience, if a little bumpy.

Trains

The Konkan Railway runs through Goa, with stations at Tivin near the beaches of North Goa, Karmali near Old Goa and Panjim, Margao in Salcette and Canacona in the far south. However, train travel is not a very convenient way to get from one part of Goa to the other, unless you are staying at a hotel near one of the railway stations.

For up-to-date details of train services, consult the bi-monthly publication the *Thomas Cook Overseas Timetable*, available to buy online at *www.thomascookpublishing.com* or from Thomas Cook branches in the UK (*tel: 01733 416477*).

Culture shock

India inevitably has a number of shocks for first-time visitors, particularly the crowds, poverty, dust and disease, but in a wealthy state like Goa, these social problems are restricted to a few areas. Although the people of Goa are used to tourists, visitors from other states of India may stare, crowd around, giggle and involve you in inane conversation out of curiosity. Do not be surprised if strangers discuss personal matters, politics and religion with you, or ask questions about your family and income:

Indians are openly curious and consider asking personal questions part of being warm and hospitable to visitors.

Bureaucratic hurdles, slow service, crowded roads and long queues can try your patience, but on the whole Goa is more relaxing and accustomed to looking after travellers than many other states in India.

Customs

In most of India, the customary greeting is to place the palms together as in prayer, and say *namaste* ('I bow to you'). Shaking hands is becoming more common, but only the most westernised Indians will shake hands with a woman. Indians use the right hand for eating and for social interactions like giving, receiving and shaking hands. It is polite to dress modestly away from the beaches, and most Indians do not smoke in front of seniors.

Photography

Many Indians are delighted to be photographed, and Goans in particular are used to it, as a result of their long exposure to tourists. However, it is still polite and prudent to ask permission of the intended subject first, particularly if it is a woman or older person. Temples and churches are the other places where caution should be exercised before snapping.

Ordinary Indians will not usually expect any payment in return for posing for your picture; the exception is at tourist sites, such as Anjuna Flea Market, where 'professional' traditional-looking photo subjects will pester you to take their picture for a small fee.

Children trying to edge their way into the frame, or curious people wanting to see your camera equipment, could crowd you, so you need to be quite tolerant.

Goa is sunny for most of the year, and there are many great opportunities to photograph 'picture-perfect' sunsets and lovely landscapes.

Camera thefts are common in India. Always take care of your camera, and do not leave it unattended in a hotel room or taxi.

Religious etiquette

Although India is a land of many religions, etiquette at most religious places is fairly standard. Visitors are expected to dress modestly and behave respectfully. You will have to take off your shoes and put out your cigarette before entering a temple or mosque. At mosques, you may have to cover your head, and women may not be allowed to enter during *namaz* (prayer times).

Women travellers

Goans are used to women tourists, but other Indian visitors may stare or make rude comments if they see western women in bathing clothes. Away from the main resorts, beaches and swimming pools, women are expected to dress sensibly and not wear bikinis, swimsuits, shorts and skimpy skirts. Most Indian women do not drink or smoke.

Goan women on their way to church

The Konkan Railway

The Konkan Railway has shortened the distance between Goa and Mumbai by about 190km (118 miles) and created a scenic rail route connecting Goa with Kerala via Mangalore.

One of the largest rail projects undertaken in post-independence India, the 760-km (472-mile) Konkan Railway was conceived as the last link in the coastal route around India, and a means to create a faster route along this section. It is regarded as an engineering marvel as it cut through hills and bridged rivers, rivulets, creeks and swamps. In all, the railway line has over 90 tunnels and more than 2,000 bridges, 171 of them major. This is a high-speed track with expectations of trains travelling at 160km (almost 100 miles) per hour, though this has not been achieved as yet.

The project was commissioned in the 1990s, and was financed by a novel method employed for the first time in India of creating a company as a joint venture of four states – Maharashtra, Goa, Karnataka and Kerala – who benefited by the construction of this project, and selling tax-free bonds. The Konkan

Railway Corporation was then given the job of creating the line and running it before handing it over to the government.

The Konkan Railway caused considerable controversy in Goa. While some looked upon it as essential to connect them to important destinations, there were groups who felt that the railway line would cause soil erosion and deforestation, affect monuments in Goa, disrupt the lives of those living along the route, impinge on the irrigation systems, and cause collection of waste-infected stagnant water resulting in mosquito-borne diseases. There were also concerns about the loose soil on the route, which could cause landslides resulting in accidents and blockages (the latter fear would prove founded in 2003, when a landslide derailed an express train, killing 51 people).

An inquiry was convened by the High Court, but the judge allowed the project to continue with minor amendments. The trains started running in 1998 and have been running since, though the ride has not been smooth, especially in the monsoon when landslides have blocked tracks. On the other hand, Konkan Railway Corporation takes pride in its use of an anti-Collision Device, a track Identification System, and a Self Stabilising Track System. Future plans include a Sky-bus metro for Goa and other destinations on the Konkan Railway line, although little progress has been made in recent years.

For travellers, the Konkan Railway has shortened the distance to Goa from Mumbai, which is the international gateway, and also made it convenient to travel economically to popular destinations like Mangalore and Cochin from Goa.

The route from Roha in Maharashtra to Mangalore in Karnataka passes through some breathtaking scenery, and the train offers views of the sea, broad rivers, paddy fields and the Western Ghats at different places.

www.konkanrailway.com

Some of the exotic scenery that can be viewed from the Konkan Railway

Central Goa

While the hippies and partygoers head north and the R&R brigade go south, Central Goa is home to far more than just the airport. Many of Goa's historical, cultural and retail highlights are found mid-state. There's also a fair complement of natural attractions, with a smattering of the golden beaches that bring the tourists in elsewhere. All this make it well worth hanging around for a while rather than simply landing and making a beeline for the resorts.

Most notably, Central Goa has two capitals – one current, one historical. Visit the former, Panaji, for a laid-back take on India's urban experience (a rare thing), its nightlife (yes, there is even gambling) and culture. Factor in a day trip to the former capital, Old Goa, to marvel at possibly the most imposing collection of churches and cathedrals ever seen in one small area. Absorbing spice farms and temples are clustered around Ponda, and those hankering after some nature can unwind at their choice of wildlife sanctuary or island, which belie their position so close to the main action.

Panaji is 26km (16 miles) from Dabolim Airport and has good road connections to the railway stations of Goa.

PANAJI

It's a great pity that many tourists, particularly those on package deals, whiz through Goa's capital and head straight for its beach resorts, as Panaji is a charming city, an easily navigable microcosm of the striking architecture,

laid-back lifestyle and cultural attractions that make the state such a popular holiday destination. Its relative cosmopolitanism affords a pleasant change from Goa's typical sand-between-your-toes resorts and bucolic villages. Days can be rounded off with a good meal, some drinks or even – unusually for India – a flutter at the table.

Part of Panaji's (which you may still hear referred to by its European name Panjim) easygoing pleasantness comes from the river than runs through it. Though some of the vessels that ply the Mandovi are going about industrial business, the waterway is more given to leisure pursuits, with sunset cruises, rambunctious party boats and even floating casinos adding to the good-time vibe. Having a large body of water in the vicinity also means that some of your journeys will be made by ferry, another agreeable facet of city life. Few of the hassles that blight many of the large Indian cities – grinding poverty, frenzied traffic, irritating street scams, over-insistent vendors – will register on your radar here. Panaji, with its compact size and unhurried pace of life, doesn't even have the feel of a capital city (it is not even the state's largest), although its sophisticated cultural, gastronomic and night-time scene certainly do.

Much of the town's character comes from its Portuguese heritage. Once a marshy island home to a few fishing villages, it gained military importance under Muslim rule, when the sultan set about building five forts and a palace.

This architectural booty caught the eye of the European invaders, and Alfonso de Albuquerque soon co-opted the town into a Portuguese stronghold. But their focus lay elsewhere, and Panaji did not become the capital until 1843. Thus ennobled, the city was duly prettified, but Goa's importance to the Portuguese was by then on the wane, so development was relatively modest. Walking around the town now, with its wide boulevards and cosy houses, you may conclude that this has worked out to be in Panaji's favour.

Central Goa

Central Goa

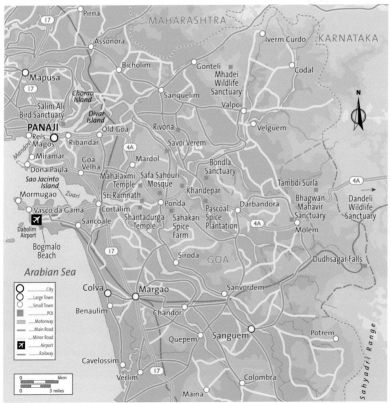

Church of Our Lady of the Immaculate Conception

Originally built in 1540, this church served as a landmark for the ship crews entering the Mandovi river estuary, and as a place to offer thanks for a safe landing. It was rebuilt in 1619 after becoming a parish church in 1600. Situated in a beautiful square of Panaji, a distinctive feature of the church is the impressive, four-tiered zigzag staircase, built in the 18th century when land was reclaimed in front of the building. Its arches were strengthened to bear the weight of the huge golden bell which was moved here in 1871 from St Augustine's Church. The church has an altar to Our Lady of the Immaculate Conception, flanked by two ornate altars to Jesus the Crucified and to Our Lady of the Rosary, with marble statues of St Paul and St Peter on either side (*see p40*).

Church Square, Jose Falcao Road, near Government of India Tourist Office, Panaji. Open: daily 9am–7pm. Free admission.

Goa State Museum

The state archaeology museum building exhibits Hindu and Jain sculpture, bronzes and inscriptions, a Christian art collection, terracottas and paintings from around India donated by S K Banerji (who was governor of Goa), musical instruments, religious objects, an ethnological collection called the Cultural Anthropology Gallery, a section on environment and conservation, Kadamba coins, photographs of the freedom struggle of Goa, porcelain, contemporary art of India and *azulejos* (hand-painted tiles). On the first floor is the ornate table used for the Inquisition, with the high-backed chairs of the Inquisitors.

The impressive façade of the 16th-century Church of Our Lady of the Immaculate Conception

Idalcao Palace

Goa State Museum, near Kadamba Bus Stand. Tel: 2438006.
www.goamuseum.nic.in.
Open: Mon–Fri 9.30am–5.30pm.
Closed: public holidays. Free admission.

Idalcao Palace

This was the castle of the Sultan of Bijapur, Yusuf Adil Shah, who the Portuguese called Idalcao. The building has been completely revamped, so it looks like a Portuguese colonial structure with sloping tiled roof, wooden verandas and coat of arms sculpted in stone. It became the Viceregal Palace from 1754 and the administrative hub of Panaji when the Viceroy moved residence to Cabo Raj Niwas in 1918. After Goa became part of India in 1961, the Idalcao Palace was the first secretariat with the Indian Ashoka Chakra symbol replacing the Portuguese emblem. Today, it houses government offices, and is undergoing extensive renovation.

In a small square near the Idalcao Palace is the statue of Abbé Faria, an 18th-century priest, in the process of hypnotising a woman. Considered a major contributor to the modern concept of psychology, Abbé Faria insisted that hypnosis was the result of suggestion and not produced by fluids. Born in Candolim, Faria studied in Lisbon and moved to Paris where his interest in hypnosis developed. His courses and 'performances' attracted a large following, but they were denounced by the clergy and even the scientific community, especially as many of his students and patients were women. This brought an end to his career, although his book on the causes of lucid sleep was published around the time of his death in 1819.

Across the road from the palace is the mansion of the Mhamai Kamat family who owned a large brokering house. This mansion is considered one of the finest surviving Hindu buildings in Panaji.
Near the main boat terminus of Panaji.

Institute Menezes Braganza

This institute was established in 1871 to encourage literary and scientific interests among the people of Goa. Originally called Vasco da Gama Institute, it was renamed after Menezes Braganza, an important figure in Goa's struggle for freedom against the Portuguese. The entrance hall has blue tiles hand-painted by Jorge Colaço in 1935, set in a clockwise frieze depicting the mythical story of the Portuguese conquest of Goa. This leads to India's oldest public library, which houses a large collection of priceless books. Upstairs there's an art gallery exhibiting European and Goan paintings, rare prints and a table dating from the time of the Inquisition.
Malaca Road, near the Police headquarters. Tel: 2436327. Open: Mon–Fri 9.30am– 1.15pm & 2–5.45pm. Closed: public holidays. Free admission.

The old colonial quarters

Fontainhas is an interesting old area of Panaji, with terracotta-tiled houses set along narrow streets and climbing up Altinho hill. The houses are generally modest, with neoclassical façades and verandas, and some have retained their ochre, yellow, blue and green coats of paint which date from the days when the Portuguese insisted that only churches could be painted white. The quarter takes its name from *Fonte Phoenix*, a natural spring, and the water supply was further enhanced by a reservoir. The white-washed Chapel of St Sebastian has a crucifix that once hung in the Palace of the Inquisition, and then the Viceregal Palace, before it was brought here.

The adjoining old quarter is San Tome, named after the square where public executions took place during the 1787 Pinto Revolt (*see p9*).
West of Ourem Creek. Buses go to Fontainhas from the centre of Panaji.

Hand-painted tiles at Panaji Library

View towards Cabo Raj Niwas from Dona Paula

PANAJI ENVIRONS
Dona Paula

A popular beach excursion for travellers staying in Panaji, Dona Paula is named after a woman whose tomb is in the chapel of Cabo Raj Niwas, and who is generally believed to be a viceroy's daughter who flung herself off the cliff here because she could not marry a local fisherman, Vaspar Dias. Dona Paula is said to have bequeathed the land to the church here. At the pier is a sculpture called *Images of India* designed by the late Baroness Yrsa von Leistner.

Dona Paula is 7km (4¼ miles) west of Panaji.

Goa Velha

Goa Velha is believed to be the original Govapuri, founded by the Kadamba ruler from present-day Chandor to control trade in the area. It was said to be a major international port and a centre for trade with Arabia and Southeast Asia. The port went into decline because it silted up, and it was destroyed by the Bahmani Muslims in the early 1470s. The Portuguese named this area, one of their oldest conquests in India, Goa Velha to distinguish it from their capital, Velha Goa or Old Goa.

Today, Goa Velha is largely deserted, but the surrounding villages have some fine churches. The 18th-century Church of St Lawrence at Agassaim has a heavily gilded altar with a richly decorated rococo reredos and a chancel with an attractive ceiling. Agassaim celebrates the Franciscan Procession of All Saints at St Andrew's Church.

The **Pilar Seminary**, a monastery established in 1613 by the Capuchin monks and named after the statue of Our Lady of Pilar which was brought from Spain, remains a centre of religious education. After the Capuchins were expelled from Goa in 1835, the Seminary and Our Lady of Pilar Church were taken over by Carmelites in 1858, who restored the abandoned buildings, and later it became the headquarters of the Missionary Society of St Xavier.

The **Church of Our Lady of Pilar** has an impressive Baroque façade, with a gable inscribed with the seminary's foundation date of 1613. The entrance porch is lined with Portuguese tombstones and near it is the tomb of Father Agnelo D'Souza, who headed the seminary from 1918 to 1927 and is revered by worshippers as a *de facto* saint for his dedicated service. The church has a number of old statues and the relatively recent chapel has a marble altar, fine paintings and stained glass, with a good view from the first floor.

The seminary also has a museum (*Open: Mon–Sat 8am–1pm & 3–6pm; admission free*) housing sculptures and terracotta items found in the gardens (which are believed to belong to the Goveshwar Shiva Temple that existed at this site and gave Goa its name), the Kadamba's lion symbol, a bas-relief of St Mary Magdalene and a Marathi translation of the Gospels.

North of Pilar is the **Church of St Anne**, known locally as Santana, at Talaulim. The church is said to have been founded in the 16th century after reports that Santana had appeared here, and was then replaced in 1695 by the present building. This was the parish church with a large congregation, but it fell into disrepair when Old Goa declined and the seat of power shifted to Nova Goa or Panaji. But despite the dilapidation, the Baroque façade is still

The courtyard at the Pilar Seminary

The brightly coloured roofs of the Maruti Temple (*see p41*)

impressive and the church is regarded as one of the finest examples of Indian Baroque in Goa. Inside the church are an imposing reredos and carved wooden pulpit. The church hosts a feast in July, which is attended by both Christians and Hindus who come to seek the blessings of the Virgin Mary. The church is not generally kept open, but it is sometimes possible to ring the bell or enquire locally to have it unlocked.
Goa Velha is 9km (5½ miles) southeast of Panaji.

Miramar

A very pleasant stroll (or a bus ride) from the centre of Panaji along Dayanand Bandodkar Marg is Miramar, home to the city's nearest beach. It's mostly the locals who venture into the water, tourists tend to stick to promenading and watching the sun go down. There are plenty of food stalls, or for something a bit more self-indulgent you could pop into the Marriott Hotel.

Xavier Centre of Historical Research

The Xavier Centre of Historical Research (XCHR) focuses on historical research into the Portuguese colonial period and houses an important library and documentation centre of books, papers and manuscripts. This Jesuit-run centre has conducted international and national seminars on Indo-Portuguese history, Jesuit and Asian studies, and holds local seminars and lectures on a regular basis. The centre's museum is known for its collection of 16th- to 18th-century Christian art, and it houses paintings by the late Angelo da Fonseca and other artists, statues, palm-leaf manuscripts, commemorative medallions, stone inscriptions, Kadamba coins, a Maratha edict and antiques.
BB Borkar Road, Alto Porvorim. Tel: 2417772. www.xchr.in. Open: Mon–Fri 9am–1pm & 2–5pm, Sat 9.30am–1pm. Free admission.

Walk: Panaji's Latin Quarter

This 4.5km (3-mile) walk explores Fontainhas, perhaps the most charming neighbourhood of Goa, with blocks of ochre, blue, light yellow and green Portuguese colonial-period houses set along Altinho Hill. It also takes in the main places of worship and other historical buildings for a good overview of Panaji's attractions.

Allow 2 hours, including walking and sightseeing time.

1 Church of Our Lady of the Immaculate Conception

See p34.

Walk east on Emidio Gracia Road or Corte de Oiterio, built in the 1870s and 1880s, to a junction where fruit vendors usually stand with their barrows in front of a two-storey 19th-century house. *Turn right onto 31 Janeiro Road. About 150m (500ft) after the junction comes*

Park Lane Lodge, beside which are the laterite steps leading to the High Court of Mumbai.

2 High Court of Mumbai

The High Court of Mumbai (Bombay) functions in Goa from a complex of buildings that once comprised the Lyceum school campus. The court building is one of the best-preserved

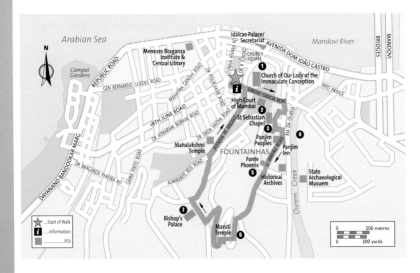

mid-19th-century historical landmarks of Goa, with a high-pitched tiled roof, elegant windows, arched entrances and mature palm trees.

Tel: 2232070. Open: Mon–Fri 10.30am–1.30pm & 2.30–4.30pm. Closed: Sat & Sun. Free admission.
Return to Park Lane Lodge and turn right for the St Sebastian Chapel.

3 St Sebastian Chapel

This white-washed chapel was built in the 1880s, replacing a smaller one built earlier in the same century to house statues and relics moved here from other churches. The highlight of the chapel is the huge crucifix brought from the Palace of the Inquisition in Old Goa. It is a lifelike depiction of Jesus with head held up and eyes open – it is said to have been designed to inspire fear and remorse in those being interrogated.

Near the chapel is a 19th-century mansion that houses the office of the delegation of the Fundação Oriente (*tel: 2230728, email: foriente@dataone.in*), a Portuguese foundation for cultural, educational, artistic, scientific, philanthropic and social projects. The building houses a small exhibition gallery, library and internet café.
Return to 31 Janeiro Road.

4 Panjim Inn and Panjim Peoples

Panjim Inn is an 1880s mansion converted into a heritage hotel and art gallery. The Panjim Peoples, the schoolhouse opposite, is also a heritage hotel.

31 Janeiro Road. Tel: 2226523. www.panjiminn.com. Open: 9am–6pm. Free admission.
Take the right fork to Fonte Phoenix.

5 Fonte Phoenix

A stepped reservoir with a fountain that is said to have spouted a phoenix, giving it the name.
The same road continues to the steps of the Maruti Temple.

6 Maruti Temple

This temple has a colourful façade and good views from its veranda. At night, when lit up, it is quite spectacular.
Tel: 2426090. Open: 7am–9pm. Free admission.
The road behind the temple leads up Altinho Hill to the Bishop's Palace.

7 Bishop's Palace

Built in the 1880s and 1890s, the residence of the Archbishop of Goa and Daman is a huge and imposing white mansion with a silver-painted Jesus. It is not open to the public.
Walk to the junction and then turn right on the road heading downhill to Church Square.

Colourful old houses in Fontainhas

OLD GOA AND DIVAR

More like a kind of religious theme park than an actual town, a visit to Old Goa, once the capital of Portuguese India, is something of a surreal experience. A scattering of churches with little in between them, the place has the feel of a ghost town – ironic because it is a hugely popular tourist destination. Divar Island, meanwhile, is a slice of bucolic Goa close to the former and current capitals.

The spectacular rise and fall of Old Goa's fortunes lie behind its odd feel. Few towns have such dramatic histories. In its heyday, Velha Goa was one of the world's largest cities. Famous for its riches and splendour, in the 16th century it was home to 200,000 people – more than Lisbon or London. Dubbed 'the Rome of the East', it also attracted comparisons with Amsterdam. But the city was plagued – literally. Epidemics of cholera, malaria and other tropical diseases repeatedly decimated the population, eventually persuading the Portuguese to seek an alternative capital. In the 1840s Old Goa was abandoned, cementing its decline from illustrious metropolis to the desolate curiosity it is today. But while many of its buildings fell into ruin, those that survived and were restored are impressive enough for the site to fully justify its status as a World Heritage Site.

Archaeological Museum

The Franciscan convent at the back of St Francis Church was converted into an archaeological museum in 1964. The main hallway is dominated by a 16th-century bronze statue of Alfonso de Albuquerque. To its left is the key gallery with sculpture from Hindu sites, many dating to the 12th and 13th centuries when Kadamba, Chalukya, Vijayanagara and Hoysala rulers flourished in Goa and neighbouring Karnataka, including an impressive one of Lord Vishnu, depicting his ten reincarnations above his head, with his consort Lakshmi and his eagle mount Garuda. There's also an interesting collection of hero stones commemorating naval and other battles, sati memorial stones, and a bronze sculpture of poet Luis Vaz de Camões holding his epic, written while he was in Goa.

On the first floor is a portrait gallery featuring paintings of Portuguese governors from Dom João de Castro in 1527 to Salazar who governed during Goa's freedom struggle, showing changing styles of Portuguese courtly dress. The old monastic cells now house sculptures and inscriptions.

West of Se Cathedral. Tel: 2285302.
Open: Sat–Thur 10am–5pm.
Closed: Fri. Admission charge.

Basilica of Bom Jesus

This church is renowned for the tomb of St Francis Xavier, follower of St Ignatius Loyola, who founded the Jesuit Order. Construction was completed in 1605 and the Renaissance façade shows Doric, Ionic and Corinthian design elements. Prominently displayed on the façade is the Jesuit emblem with the letters IHS, an abbreviation for Jesus, saviour of Men. Inside, the Basilica has a massive gilt altar, a richly ornamented reredos with gold-leaf work, scrolls, carved panels, statues and illuminated pilasters, and a memorial of Dom Jeromina Mascarenhas who financed the church through his will.

The main attraction for most visitors who come to the church, however, is the three-tiered tomb of St Francis Xavier, gifted to the Basilica by the Grand Duke of Tuscany in exchange for a pillow on which the saint's head is said to have rested. It took the sculptor Giovanni Batista Foggini a decade to design the tomb and the silver casket in which the saint's remains are housed. Made from marble and inlaid with jasper, the elaborate casket has well-crafted bronze plaques depicting St Francis Xavier preaching, baptising converts, escaping natives by swimming, and on his deathbed.

A corridor leads from the tomb to the Sacristy which has a superbly carved wooden door and relics from the life of St Francis Xavier, a room housing modern art and a gallery with a good view of the tomb.

Next to the Basilica is the Professed House of the Jesuits, from where missions were organised.
Near Mahatma Gandhi statue. Open: Mon–Sun 6.30am–6.30pm. English Mass Sun 10.15am. Free admission.

The multi-styled façade of the Basilica of Bom Jesus

St Francis Xavier

For Roman Catholics, St Francis Xavier's association with Goa and his remains are the principal treasures of the state. He was born in April 1506 into a wealthy and noble family in Navarre, which is now part of Spain. After studying theology and philosophy in Paris, he was recruited by Ignatius Loyola into the Society of Jesus.

Francis Xavier was sent to Goa to work in the diocese that comprised a vast area east of the Cape of Good Hope. He arrived as a 35-year-old in 1542, and remained here for a brief spell as a teacher, before moving further south. He left a deep imprint on religious life in Goa and Kerala, founding many churches and converting thousands of people.

Xavier's missions took him to Southeast Asia. On his journey back to India, he stopped at Sancian, off the China coast, and died on the island in December 1552. When he was buried, a companion put lime into his coffin. When his body was eventually exhumed and carried to Malacca it was still fresh and had been unaffected by the lime, which normally hastens decomposition. Reburied in Malacca, the body was taken to Goa in 1554, where its incorruptible condition was considered a miracle. On examination, it was found that the body had not been embalmed and the internal organs remained intact. The mortal remains have been venerated by Catholics ever since.

Clear instructions are given at the head of the queue to see the body of St Francis Xavier

The mummified body of the Saint attracts pilgrims from all over the world

First housed in St Paul's College, Francis Xavier's remains were moved to Bom Jesus Basilica in Old Goa. He was beatified in 1619 and declared a Saint in 1622, by which time the right arm, shoulder blades and internal organs had been divided among Jesuits elsewhere. In 1635 the body was moved to its chapel where it is still entombed today. An interesting permanent display on St Francis, with a video presentation, maps of his travels and other biographical information, is now hosted in the library next to the Basilica of Bom Jesus (*Open: 9am–5pm*).

EXPOSITIONS

After his canonisation, St Francis Xavier's body was exposed for viewing on each anniversary of his death, but this ceased after damage was caused to his body in the early 1700s. However, official expositions resumed in order to dispel rumours that the Jesuits had taken the body when they were expelled from Goa in the 1750s. Since 1859, the body has been on view every 10 or 12 years on the anniversary of his death or on various special occasions. Since 1953 pilgrims have not been allowed to touch the remains and can only view it in a crystal container. The last exposition was in 2004–5, when an estimated 2.2 million pilgrims visited Old Goa, and the next is scheduled for November 2014.

Se Cathedral

The largest church in Old Goa, and said to be the largest in Asia, Se Cathedral is dedicated to St Catherine on whose day in 1510 Old Goa was captured by Albuquerque. King Dom Sebastiao commissioned the building of the cathedral in 1562 on the site of the older church commissioned by Albuquerque, and it took 90 years to complete. Though it was built by Dominicans, the cathedral is largely Tuscan and Corinthian in style. The remaining tower has the Golden Bell, which is one of Asia's largest and is known for the richness of its tone.

The cathedral has a large central nave with four attractive chapels along the aisles, and a double-vaulted ceiling. The main altar is beautifully decorated and the reredos towering over it has carved and gilded panels depicting scenes from the life of St Catherine, including her interaction with Roman emperor Maxim who wanted to marry her, her martyrdom and her headless body being carried by angels. The Chapel of the Blessed Sacrament is also gilded, the Chapel of the Cross of Miracles, behind a richly carved wooden screen, is believed to cure sickness, the altar of St Anne houses

Cannon in the grounds of the Church of St Francis of Assisi, Old Goa (see p48)

Se Cathedral is beautifully constructed in a fusion of Tuscan and Corinthian styles

relics of the Blessed Martyrs of Cuncolim who were executed for trying to convert people from the Mughal court, and the chapel near the entrance has the font that was made in 1532 and said to have been used by St Francis Xavier.

The Chapel of St Catherine stands in the same square as Se Cathedral. The chapel has a twin-towered façade that is believed to have been the prototype for the Goan church architecture that began with Se Cathedral.

Off Rua Direita. Open: Mon–Sun 6.30am–6pm. Free admission.

Divar Island

Connected by ferry to Old Goa, Divar's main attraction is the **Church of Our Lady of Compassion** – a rebuilt version of the older Lady Divar Church, which dated from 1699–1724 – ascribed to Fr Antonio João de Frias, an architect and a writer.

The church has an impressive Baroque façade, and its interior is decorated with attractive stuccowork, Baroque plaster decorations and altars. *Approached by ferry from the Old Goa jetty near Arch of the Viceroys, Naroa and Ribander.*

Walk: Churches in Old Goa

The best way to see the monuments of Old Goa is by following this 1.2km (¾-mile) walking route.

Start at the Arch of the Viceroys near the ferry for Divar and walk to St Cajetan Church, on the left-hand side of the road.

Allow 4–5 hours, including walking time and sightseeing.

1 St Cajetan Church

Built in 1661 by the friars of the Theatine Order, which was founded by St Cajetan, this church is modelled on St Peter's Basilica in Rome. The façade has imposing Corinthian columns, niches with statues of the Apostles flanking the doors, and one of the few church domes in Goa. Inside, the vaulted ceiling displays floral patterns, while the main altar has an elaborately decorated reredos and equally attractive side altars.
Walk from St Cajetan Church towards the intersection with Mahatma Gandhi's statue. Just before the intersection, on the right, is the side entrance to Se Cathedral.

2 Se Cathedral

See pp46–7.
Walk west, past the Archbishop's Palace, to St Francis of Assisi Church in the same complex as the cathedral.

3 St Francis of Assisi Church

One of the most interesting churches in Goa, this church was founded as a chapel by the Franciscan Friars in 1527. The present structure dates from 1661 but retains the original ornate doorway. The church has a beautiful interior with heavily gilded walls and ceiling, paintings on wood depicting the life of St Francis, carved wood panels, an arch decorated with floral murals and an exquisite carved pulpit.

There are four statues of the Apostles in the reredos and above it are large figures of Christ on the Cross and St Francis standing on the three Franciscan vows of 'Poverty, Humility and Obedience'. Like many other Goan churches, this one too has Portuguese tombstones on the floor of the nave.

Next to the church is the Archbishop's Palace, which is unique as one of the last surviving civil buildings of Goa Dourada, the golden age of Old Goa, and now houses the Kristu Kala Mandir Art Gallery (*Open: Tues–Sun 9.30am–5.30pm. Free admission*).
Open: Mon–Sun 9am–5.30pm. Free admission. Cross the road from the gate

of the Se Cathedral complex to the
Basilica of Bom Jesus.

4 Basilica of Bom Jesus

See pp42–3.
*Exit the Basilica on the taxi stand side and
ascend the 'holy hill' of Santa Monica.*

5 Convent of Santa Monica

Built in 1606, and subsequently
rebuilt after a fire in 1636, this was the
first nunnery in India. It was
abandoned in 1885 when the last
sister died, and it is now used as a
theological centre and a college for
nuns. A part of the building houses the
Museum of Christian Art, with more
than 150 exhibits collected from
churches and Christian homes. On the

other side of the road is the Monastery
of St John of God, which opened in the
18th century and is now a home for
senior citizens.
*Museum open: 9.30am–5pm. Nominal
admission charge.*
*Follow the road from the monastery to
the tower of the Church of St Augustine.*

6 Tower of the Church of St Augustine

A tall tower is all that is left of this
church, built in 1602 by Augustinian
friars. The church was abandoned in
1835 because of the Portuguese
repressive attitude to the Orders.
*From the tower retrace your steps to the
Basilica on the main road for transport
back to Panaji.*

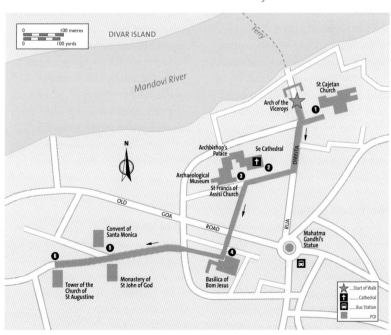

PONDA

Tourists come to Ponda for two reasons: temples and spices. The industrial town serves as a jumping off point for a collection of noteworthy places of worship, built to preserve idols from the marauding Portuguese. Several spice farms in the area provide enjoyable insights into India's vast world of seasonings. The bustling town also makes a break from Goa's languid resorts, offering a glimpse of the state going about its daily business.

Khandepar

Some of the oldest monuments of Goa, the cave temples of Khandepar are set beside a rivulet, a tributary of the Mandovi. The caves are believed to have been occupied by Buddhist monks and to have been converted into Hindu cave temples by the Kadambas in the 10th–11th-century period when the stepped roofs were added. Each of the caves has a pair of cells with pegs for robes and utensils, and niches for oil lamps, and one of them has the Kadambas' lotus motif.

5km (3 miles) northeast of Ponda on National Highway 4.

Mahalaxmi Temple

Though this is one of the plainest of the temples in and around Ponda, it has a large congregation because Mahalaxmi was considered the mother goddess of the world by the Kadamba and other dynasties. The Mahalaxmi idol here depicts a peaceful image of this goddess of the Shakti, or power culture, like the one at Kolhapur (*see pp114–15*) which is the most important place for her worship, and has a lingam (symbol of Shiva) on her head.

Open: 6am–8.30pm. Admission charge. 4km (2¹/₂ miles) northwest of Ponda in Bandora village.

Safa Shahouri Mosque

Goa's largest and oldest mosque, Safa Shahouri, was built by Ali Adil Shah and was said to rival those of Bijapur, but the buildings were damaged when the Portuguese conquered Ponda, and subsequently fell into neglect. What remains is, however, an unusual and interesting building, with the rectangular prayer room standing on a high plinth. The mosque has a pointed pitched roof in the local style and cusped Bijapuri arches, some of which frame the windows, while others are purely decorative. The courtyard outside has the stumps of columns that once supported a roof providing shade to worshippers. On the south side is a tank which is used for cleansing.

On the National Highway, 2km (1¹/₄ miles) to the northwest of Ponda town.

Savoi Verem

The Ananta Temple at Savoi Verem is dedicated to Lord Vishnu as *Sheshashahi Ananta*, the god who sits on the coils of a serpent. The temple has a reclining Vishnu in black stone, with a distinctive conical headdress,

shown before the dawn of creation with a lotus bearing Lord Brahma, the creation god, coming out of his navel. Otherwise fairly simple, the temple has colourful wooden columns and bases in the *mandapa* (main hall).
The temple is outside Savoi Verem village, about 10km (6 miles) north of Ponda.

Shantadurga Temple

This is one of Goa's largest and most visited temples, situated at Queula, southwest of the main Ponda bus stop. Built by Maratha warrior Shahu, the temple has a large tank set in the hillside, a six-storey lamp tower and a tall tower over the sanctum, while the chandelier-lit interior has polished marble floors. The main deity is a form of Durga, called Shantadurga, or the peaceful Durga, because she mediated in a very fierce battle between Vishnu and Shiva that threatened to destroy the universe. Devotees believe Brahma approached Durga, who helped settle the quarrel, bringing *shanti* (peace) back to the world. The idol of Shantadurga is flanked by Shiva and Vishnu, and the temple houses a partially gilded temple car which is used for processions. It also has an octagonal drum with a lantern, showing European Christian influences on the Hindu architecture. The temple is often packed with devotees, as Shantadurga has a large following in Goa.
At Queula, about 2km (1¹/₄ miles) off the Ponda Road.

This attractive Safa Shahouri Mosque is the legacy of Ali Adil Shah

Shri Nangesh Temple

The principal deity of the temple is Lord Shiva as Naguesh or Nangesh, lord of serpents. A tablet dates the temple to 1413, but it underwent renovation in the 18th century. The temple has a domed roof with elephant heads and peacocks at the corners, and next to its entrance porch is an imposing black Nandi (the bull mount of Lord Shiva). A noteworthy feature of the temple is the tank, full of carp, which is surrounded by palm trees and weathered stones. Another striking aspect is the *mandapa* (pavilion), which has painted woodcarvings depicting the eight guardians and illustrating tales from the Mahabharata and Ramayana epics. The lamp tower has paintings of deities near the base and Ganesh above. The main sanctum has a silver door leading to the shrines of Shiva, Lakshmi and Vishnu, and Ganesh, besides subsidiary shrines. *4km (2¹/₂ miles) northwest of Ponda in Bandora village.*

Siroda

The Kamakshi temple at Siroda is dedicated to another form of Shantadurga. The temple has a *linga*

Shri Nangesh Temple is dedicated to Shiva as lord of serpents

Mahalsa Narayani Temple near Ponda

(symbol) of Rayeisvar and the image of Lakshminarayan, brought here from other temples in Raia, which were destroyed by the Portuguese in the 16th century. The temple has an unusual pagoda-style tile-roofed tower, with serpents along the roof and four kneeling elephants at the base.
11km (7 miles) south of Ponda.

Sri Ramnath Temple

The Sri Ramnath Temple is noted for the silver screen door in front of the main shrine. The screen is opulently decorated and certainly one of the most extravagant of its kind found in Goa, in particular, the portrayal of figures worshipping a lingam and the depiction of Lord Vishnu reclining with Goddess Lakshmi on the coils of a serpent. The lingam (singular of linga) brought here from Lutolim is worshipped by both Shaivite and Vaishnavite sects because Shri Ramnath is a form of Shiva called upon by Lord Rama before his battle of Lanka.
At Queula, about 2km (1¼ miles) west of Ponda.

Tour: Temple Trail from Ponda to Priol

This 11km (7-mile) tour along the road from Ponda to Priol takes you to visit some of Goa's most famous temples.

Allow 2–3 hours for sightseeing and travel.

Start at Ponda and drive 4km (2½ miles) northwest on the NH4A to Bandora. Turn left onto a winding road which dips down from the highway to the Shri Nangesh Temple.

1 Shri Nangesh Temple
See p52.

Return to the NH4A and drive towards Farmagudi.

2 Ganesh Temple and Shivaji statue
This interesting Ganesh Temple blends medieval and contemporary styles. Opposite the temple is an equestrian

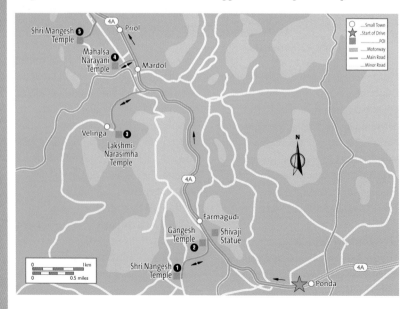

statue of Shivaji, the great Maratha ruler, who conquered Ponda Fort in 1675.

Just north of Farmagudi is the left turn for Velinga, immediately before a small river bridge.

3 Velinga

The Lakshmi-Narasimha Temple at Velinga has an image of Narasimha, the half-man half-lion image of Lord Vishnu which was brought here from Salcette, where the Portuguese destroyed many temples. Vishnu took on this form to deal with a demon to which Brahma had granted immunity from man and beast. It is a typical 18th-century temple, except for the domed tower which has some Islamic features. Inside, the *mandapa* has carved wooden columns and the main shrine has some interesting silverwork. There is a good view of the temple from the tank outside.

Return to the highway and drive north to Mardol. To the left of the highway at Mardol is the Mahalsa Narayani Temple.

4 Mahalsa Narayani Temple

The idol of Mahalsa, the Goan form of Mohini, female form of Vishnu, was rescued from a destroyed temple in Verna, Salcette, and brought to Mardol. The inner area has carved columns and paintings of the ten *avatars* (incarnations) of Vishnu, and the seven-storeyed lamp tower is lit on special occasions. An arch leads to the tank, picturesquely located among palms and paddy fields.

Return to the NH4A and drive north,

turning left for Shri Mangesh Temple on a wooded hill just off the main highway.

5 Shri Mangesh Temple

The 18th-century temple to Mangesh, an incarnation of Shiva, is one of Goa's most popular temples. The lingam was brought here from Cortalim when the Portuguese took control and started destroying temples. Previously housed in a smaller temple, the new premises were built for the lingam in the mid-18th century on land donated by an influential Hindu. The tank is supposedly the oldest part of the temple, and the lamp tower is one of the most famous in Goa; built in Indian Baroque style, it is painted white and shows interesting images. The main hall is hung with chandeliers, while the major shrine of Mangesh is behind a carved silver screen and shares the hall with shrines of Ganesh and Parvati. Nearby is the basil enclosure called *tulsi vrindavan.*

Hindu worship often involves a musical offering to the deities

Spice plantations

Goa's geography and climate make the state suitable for the growing of spices, cashews, fruits and areca nuts. Some of these plantations are located near Ponda where the landscape is part wetland and part hillside, allowing a variety of trees and plants to be cultivated at different levels. Today, many plantations offer tours during which visitors can see the techniques used to grow and harvest the spices, learn about the uses of the spices and herbs that are essential ingredients in India's cuisines and in alternative medical sciences like Ayurveda, and are given the opportunity to sample or purchase various spices. The tour fee could include a meal.

Pascoal Spice Plantation

At this plantation there are three major cash crops of coconut, cashew

The Tropical Spice Plantation at Keri

and areca nuts, with pineapple in their shade, as well as mango, papaya and jackfruit and numerous spices such as cinnamon, nutmeg, black pepper, cloves and cardamom. The plantation has bonsai of many trees, and grows ornamental flowering plants. It also has a nursery of fruit-growing species.

Pascoal Spice Plantation, Khandepar. Tel: 2344268. www.pascoalfarm.com. Open: 8am–6pm. Admission charge.

Sahakari Spice Farm

This 53-hectare (130-acre) plantation with about 24 cultivated hectares (60 acres) offers a tour that usually begins with a welcome drink of coconut milk or local juices and ends with a traditional meal. Visitors are told about the organic farming methods developed by the owners of the farm over more than 30 years, including pesticide-free cultivation, compost heaps, and the use of alternative energies like solar power, and their own methane gas production units. Pepper, nutmeg, cinnamon, cardamom, cloves, chillies and vanilla are the main spices grown, and the farm also produces coconuts, areca nuts, cashews and fruits such as papaya, mango, jackfruit, bread fruit, grapefruit, star-apple, Ayurvedic plants, tea and coffee. Guests can see the dairy with hybrid cows and the feni-distillation unit where they can also taste the locally made cashew feni.

Sahakari Spice Farm, Ponda–Belgaum Highway. Tel: 2312394. www.sahakarifarms.com. Email: info@sahakarifarms.com. Open: 9.30am–4pm; last entrance around 2pm. Admission charge.

Spices for sale at the market

Sai Organic Farm & Herbarium

This plantation has, besides spices and fruits, a strong focus on Ayurvedic plants whose uses are explained on a tour.

Abyss, Savoi-Verem, Ponda. Tel: 2340308. Admission charge.

Savoi Plantation

This plantation, now over 200 years old and covering about 40 hectares (100 acres), is owned by the Shetye family. After a traditional welcome with flowers, drink and snacks, visitors tour the plantations where they see areca nut palms, coconut palms, pepper vines, soft- and hard-skin jackfruit, banana and grapefruit plants, and hillsides planted with pineapple, bamboo, cocoa, wood apple and mango. Cinnamon, cardamom, clove and nutmeg are among the many spices grown at this plantation, which also grows cashew, papaya, chikoo and medicinal plants. The tour includes watching the local people making utensils and decorative items out of local produce like coconuts. The plantation has accommodation and meal facilities.

Savoi Plantation, Ponda. Tel: 2340272. Open: 10.30am–5pm. www.savoiplantation.com. Admission charge.

Tropical Spice Plantation

This plantation has a reception area next to a wetland where welcome drinks and lunch on banana leaves are served. During the tour, visitors see cashews, spices and other plants, and also learn about the medicinal uses of spices and Ayurvedic plants from the guide.

Tropical Spice Plantation, Arla Bazar, Keri. Tel: 2340329. Open: 9am–4pm. Admission charge.

THE WESTERN GHATS

The Sanguem *taluka* of Goa covers the forested hills that form the border areas towards Karnataka in the east. This *taluka* (district) is home to Goa's highest peaks and is inhabited by a variety of wildlife. Away from the Old Conquest areas of the Portuguese, it displays the state's oldest surviving temples and villages, where traditional handicrafts are made.

Dudhsagar Falls

Dudhsagar Falls are among the highest in India, with a drop of 310m (1,017ft), and they are at their most impressive during and soon after the monsoons. The falls – whose name means 'sea of milk' – descend in stages across boulders and down rock faces, dividing and reuniting, and forming pools on the way.
10km (6¼ miles) southeast of Molem.

Rivona

The small, roughly excavated caves of Rivona are believed to have been monastic complexes, giving the area its name Rishi Van ('the forest of monks'), which subsequently was shortened to Rivona. The finding of a Buddha statue, dating from about the 7th century, proves that this was an important Buddhist site. The caves were later taken over by Hindus who carved their deities, including Hanuman, on the walls. Today, locals call them the **Pandava Caves**, named after the Mahabharata heroes, the Pandavas, who were exiled and lived in caves.

The first cave is situated near a water pump, with steps leading down to a vestibule. It has a well, a pool near the entrance porch, and tanks that store natural spring water. The other main cave is on the valley floor not far from the river. Take a torch and beware of snakes.
2km (1¼ miles) southeast of Sanquelim.

Tambdi Surla

Tucked into the forested foothills of Sanguem, the **Mahadev Temple** is the only well-preserved structure of the Kadamba Dynasty in Goa. This small 12th- to 13th-century temple is constructed from black basalt stone that must have been transported from some distance away.

The temple stands on a plinth and is entered through a *sabhamandapa* (entrance hall) with doorways on three sides, leading to the *antralaya* (middle hall) and the *garbagriha* (sanctuary) on an east–west axis. A carved screen separates the *sabhamandapa* from the *antralaya*. Four monolith carvings support the ceiling, in the centre of which are finely carved reliefs, with a lotus flower. To the east of the temple is the river, which must have been an ideal spot for ritual cleansing.

Much of the exterior wall is plain, but there are some fine miniature examples of sculpture and relief carvings.

The *shikara* roof above the *garbagriha* has relief carvings of

Brahma, Shiva and Vishnu with their consorts, Saraswati, Uma and Kumarashakti, and there are also some excellent carved motifs near the entrance hall.

12km (7½ miles) north of Molem.

The impressive 12th-century Mahadev Temple, constructed from black basalt stone

Birdwatching in Goa

Goa features on the birdwatching itinerary of most first-time visitors to India, who want to watch the endemic birds of the humid tropical forests of southwest India that can be spotted in the foothills of the state's Western Ghats. Many of these keen birdwatching groups return with lists of 200–250 species seen over the course of a week in Goa. Those who want to squeeze in time to watch birds while holidaying in Goa will find good habitats near beaches like Baga, Sinquerem and Dona Paula. Many resorts and hotels have begun to help arrange bird guides who know the best sites and can identify the indigenous Indian birds, or taxi drivers who can take interested visitors to good bird habitats.

Among the resorts of Goa, Baga is popular with those who want to spend time birdwatching while staying at a beach hotel or riverfront resort. The forests and scrub near the river can yield sightings of crested serpent eagle, oriental honey buzzard, black eagle, Malabar grey hornbill, rufous woodpecker, black-rumped flameback, golden oriole, Tickel's blue flycatcher, paradise flycatcher, orange-headed thrush, purple-rumped and Loten's sunbirds, rose-ringed and plum-headed parakeets, flowerpeckers, rufous treepie, minivets, leafbirds, ioras, red-whiskered and other bulbuls, blue-tailed bee-eater and many other birds. Some come into the gardens of the hotels and resorts. The flooded fields near the river are frequented by open-billed stork, ibises, lapwings, plovers, herons, warblers, pipits and wagtails. The Malabar lark and the grey-necked bunting are species that many birdwatchers hope to see in Baga. Along the beaches, the marshes can be checked for painted snipe, cinnamon bittern, ibises and kingfishers.

North of Baga, Morjim is a good site for gulls and coastal wading birds like the greater and lesser sand plovers, Kentish plover and Caspian plover, and the beach is also the nesting site of sea turtles. Resorts and camps offer accommodation near the sites.

Among the sightseeing places of Goa, Fort Aguada can be explored for birds (see p78), 8km (5 miles) south of Baga, where the Indian pitta is often seen in the wooded ridges near the fort. The marshes and fields near the road to the fort have abundant birdlife, offering opportunities to see swallows, kingfishers, stints, snipes, herons, egret and barbets. The trees should be checked for owlets, barbets, shrikes, flycatchers and weaver birds.

Boat trips on the Zuari River organised for crocodile spotting are also good to see five or six species of kingfisher as well as darters, storks and ibises. For waterfowl, the Carambolim Lake southeast of Old Goa abounds with ibises, storks, herons, cormorants, pochards, resident and migrating ducks, jacanas, swamphen, pratincoles and sandpipers.

Most serious birdwatchers focus on the forests and fruiting trees around the Tambdi Surla Temple campus (see pp58–9) and the Bhagwan Mahavir Sanctuary (see p64) near Molem, where tropical moist forest birds like Sri Lankan frogmouth, Malabar grey and pied hornbills, Nilgiri wood pigeon, small sunbird, Malabar trogon, Malabar crested lark, Malabar whistling thrush, scimitar babbler and other birds typical of this type of forest habitat can be seen, as well as owls and nightjars after dusk if you are staying at one of the camps or tourist complexes in this area. In South Goa, the Cotigao Sanctuary (see p64) near Palolem Beach is also a good site for endemic bird species of the Western Ghats. Other good sites for birdwatching are around the fruit trees of the spice plantations of Ponda (see pp56–7), Bicholim and Satari.

Herons are among the many species of birds populating the Carambolim Lake

VASCO DA GAMA

Vasco da Gama lies near the Mormugao harbour along the rocky headland jutting into the sea that is one of the busiest ports between Mumbai and Mangalore on India's west coast. The presence of this port has made Vasco da Gama the largest town in Goa, and an affluent industrial area. This town is of importance to travellers as the main railway terminal of Central Goa and as the town nearest to Dabolim Airport. Nearby are beaches like Bogmalo, Hollant and Santa.

In the 17th century, Vasco da Gama was selected by the Portuguese to be their capital, replacing Old Goa. A fort was built for the purpose, with the Viceroy actually living here for some time in the 18th century. However, the idea of Vasco da Gama as capital did not materialise, and when Panaji became the capital, the fort fell into neglect and is now hardly visible among the development of new houses and industrial areas in the town.

The harbour is the scene of a World War II episode made famous by the book *Boarding Party* by James Leasor, and the Hollywood movie *Sea Wolves*. During World War II, British intelligence, through their network based in India, believed that information about ship movement was being passed to U-boats, which were able to target British ships accurately, by a radio transmitter hidden on board German ships interned in Goa. The Germans were safe in the knowledge that they were in neutral territory as Portugal was not involved in the war. Unable to intervene for fear of a political backlash, a British Special Operations Executive came up with the unconventional idea of sinking the German and Italian ships anchored at Mormugao using a team of veteran civilians from the Calcutta Light Horse Regiment who, if caught, could just claim to be on a drunken prank as they were accountants, directors and other civilians rather than a fighting unit. The raid went off as planned and the radio room on the *Ehrenfels* – the ship relaying information about the allied convoys – was destroyed, and the ships all set afire.

Bogmalo Beach

Screened by cliffs from the industrial areas and crowded residential localities of Vasco town and harbour, Bogmalo is a popular resort destination near Vasco with a good beach, watersports facilities, and no dearth of places in which to stay, eat and drink. The **Naval Aviation Museum** at Bogmalo (*tel: 5995525. Open: Tue–Sat 10am–5pm*) exhibits military aircraft and helicopters from the Fairey Firefly fighters used during World War II, as well as more recent makes and models. The galleries display photographs and information about the history of different squadrons of naval aviation in

India, and there are exhibitions of weapons, sensors and equipment.
8km (5 miles) southeast of Vasco da Gama.

Sancoale

Sancoale is where the Jesuit missions arrived in the 16th century. The **Nossa Senhora de Saude Church** was erected to commemorate their arrival (*tel: 2550763*). Much of the church was damaged by fire in the 19th century, but the splendidly decorated panels and plasterwork of the remaining façade are testament to the magnificence of the church as it was in the 1560s.
About 10km (6 miles) east of Vasco da Gama.

São Jacinto

This is a wooded island with white-washed chapels and a lighthouse.
About 7km (4^1/$_2$ miles) east of Vasco da Gama.

Statue of Father Joseph Vaz at Sancoale church

Wildlife reserves of Goa

Although Goa is India's smallest state, its diversity of landscapes from the coast to the moist forested hills of the Western Ghats in the east has endowed it with six sanctuaries and one national park. (*See pp134–6 for contact details.*)

Bhagwan Mahavir Sanctuary

This sanctuary (also spelt Bhagwan Mahaveer) covers an area of approximately 240sq km (93sq miles) and has an impressive checklist of mammals, including panther, sloth bear, sambar and barking deer. Tigers are known to venture in at night, and even elephants come from the Karnataka border. Mouse deer, pangolin, civet, slender loris and flying squirrel are also recorded. However, all of these are rarely spotted, and over a couple of drives into the sanctuary visitors usually get to see the odd gaur (Indian bison), spotted deer, wild boar, langur and bonnet monkeys and striped neck mongoose. The sanctuary, and its surrounding area, is rich in birds, with some of the key species being Malabar hornbill, Malabar trogon, blue-eared kingfisher, Nilgiri wood pigeon, frogmouth, blue-bearded bee-eaters, Malabar whistling and blue rock thrushes, Malabar parakeets, grey jungle fowl and red spurfowl.

The sanctuary entrance is near the Molem crossroads, where there are places to stay and eat. Molem is also the starting point for hikes to Dudhsagar Falls, Atoll Gad, Matkonda Hill and Tambdi Surla.

Bondla Sanctuary

This tiny 8sq km (3sq mile) sanctuary has a zoological park as its focal point. The sanctuary has a long checklist of mammals, but there are few chances of spotting any except monkeys, the odd deer and the Malabar giant squirrel because of the volume of visitors to the zoo. Bondla is good for birdwatching, with hornbills, crested serpent eagle, black eagle, cuckoos and woodpeckers among the many species usually seen over a day or two spent in the sanctuary.

Cotigao Sanctuary

This 105 sq km (40 sq mile) sanctuary comprises moist deciduous forests, with hills to the south and east, and the Talpona River flowing through the reserve. Like the Bhagwan Mahavir Sanctuary, there is a long list of mammals recorded by the forest department brochures here, such as tiger, panther, sloth bear, gaur, sambar, barking deer, spotted deer, slender loris and flying squirrel, but sightings are not easy in the forests. This is a good area for nature treks and birdwatching, with some species being easier to spot here than elsewhere in Goa. Watchtowers at treetop levels offer an opportunity to watch birds in the canopies, and the watchtowers overlook waterholes where mammals may be seen coming to drink water. The forests of Cotigao have the villages of Kunbis and Velpis, where livestock is herded on the hillsides.

Langur monkeys are a common sight at Bhagwan Mahavir Sanctuary

Dandeli Wildlife Sanctuary

This sanctuary in Karnataka, near the Goa border, comprises moist deciduous, semi-evergreen and teak forests. They are inhabited by tiger, leopard, elephant, sloth bear, gaur, wild boar, a variety of deer, wild dog, slender loris and other mammals, and birds such as the Malabar pied hornbill, Nilgiri wood pigeon, blue-winged parakeet, and a small sunbird characteristic of the semi-evergreen forests of the Western Ghats.

Mhadei Wildlife Sanctuary

The Mhadei Valley is well known for its reptiles, such as the pit vipers, geckos and agamas. It is best known as a site for birdwatching and butterfly spotting because of the richness of the forests and the Mhadei River basin flora. The ruby-throated yellow bulbul, Nilgiri wood pigeon, blue-winged parakeet, Malabar grey hornbill and other birds characteristic of the humid forests of the Western Ghats have been seen here.

Salim Ali Bird Sanctuary

This sanctuary forms a part of Chorao Island, which is a prime birdwatching area. The banks of the island along the River Mandovi offer opportunities to see storks, herons, ducks and wading birds. The mangrove marshes of Chorao also harbour crabs and mudskipper fish.

Southern Goa

Less hectic than its northern counterpart, the south of the state has a more leisurely, traditional feel. That's not to say that the foreign incursion has left it untouched – several luxury hotels operate in the south and all the resorts dotted along the coast attract their fair share of holidaymakers, from India and overseas. But paddy fields and rustic villages punctuate the tourist infrastructure. These, along with the region's main transport hub, bustling Margao, make Southern Goa a good choice to combine beach fun with authentic India.

MARGAO

The lively market town of Margao (officially called Madgaon) is a major transport hub, but its scruffy charm makes it worth spending some time here, rather than just heading off to the next destination. Margao doesn't really do tourism, so it offers a refreshingly authentic version of Goan life that makes a change from the beach resorts. Retail opportunities are one draw – the covered market here is one of the most visited in the state, and you won't find a tie-dyed hippie skirt for love nor money. Some pretty Portuguese architecture and temples pre-dating that period are other reasons to stop off.

Church of the Holy Spirit

This typically Goan church, with a Baroque façade and ornate archway, was built in 1675 and replaced earlier versions damaged by the Muslims. In front of the church is a piazza cross carved with images of the Easter story that is among the most impressive in Goa and dominates the square. The façade of the church is considered to be one of the best examples of Baroque architecture, with a pair of square towers surmounted by domes. The interior is impressive with a gilded pulpit and stucco ceiling. The highlight of the church is an impressively carved reredos dedicated to the Virgin Mary with a gilded and carved archway in front of it. Statues of St Anthony and of the Blessed Joseph Vaz (*see p68*) are housed in glass cabinets.

The Feast of Our Lady of the Immaculate Conception is celebrated in December with a large fair at the church square.
Church Square, Margao. www. holyspiritchurchgoa.com. Open: 6.30am– noon & 4–9.30pm. Admission charge.

Colonial houses

Margao has many old houses, most of them on or near Rua Abade Faria. The Da Silva House near the Church Square is locally called the *Sat Burnzam Gor*

(House of Seven Gables) and referred to as the Casa Grande. This is a large and elegant house, though only three of the seven gables that gave it its nickname survive. It has a beautiful rococo façade featuring ornate wrought-iron balconies, decorative scrolls and oyster-shell windows. Still a private residence, it has a reputation for its carved rosewood furniture, chandeliers, mirrors, porcelain, sumptuous furniture, murals, marble floors, silverware and fine terracotta busts, but is not officially open to visitors and permission has to be obtained prior to visiting the house. *Contact the GTDC.* *www.goa-tourism.com*

MARGAO ENVIRONS

Within easy reach of Margao are the interesting villages of the Christian belt of Salcette (*see pp70–1*), known for their stately homes, the beaches favoured by upmarket resort promoters, and temples and caves in the hills.

Beaches

Salcette has a broad stretch of beach which is home to some of Goa's best-known luxury resorts and five-star hotels. This area is usually less crowded than the north coast, and it is easily accessible from most of the nearby hotels and resorts such as Velsao,

Southern Goa

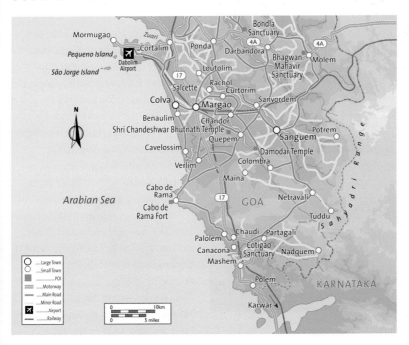

Arossim, Utorda, Majorda, Betalbatim, Colva, Benaulim, Varca, Fatarde, Cavelossim and Mobor. Fishing villages line the coast near the beaches, and the local towns and villages, such as Utorda, have a number of interesting old houses that can be seen from the road.

Benaulim

The **Church of St John of the Baptist**
(*tel: 2780555. Open: daily 9am–noon. Free admission*) is located on a hill outside Benaulim village. Built in 1596, it has an

Shri Chandeshwar Bhutnath Temple

impressive gable façade and towers surmounted by domes. Inside, the church has a well-decorated altar and an ornate pulpit, as well as representations of the Lamb of Apocalypse from the biblical book of *Revelation*, and St Christopher carrying a child.

Benaulim is the birthplace of Father Joseph Vaz, who worked for the poor, downtrodden and Goan clergy before moving to Sri Lanka where he was known as the Apostle of Ceylon. He was baptised in the chapel of the church in 1651.

Benaulim is 7km (4¼ miles) west of Margao. Frequent buses from Margao. Good stretches of beach are accessible from Benaulim village.

Colva

En route from Margao to Colva, the **Church of Our Lady of Mercy** (*tel: 2788512. Free admission*) dates from 1630 but was almost entirely rebuilt in the 18th century. On one wall is a special altar with a small figure of Menino Jesus, who has a unique place in the history of the church. The original Menino Jesus image was brought here by a Jesuit father from Mozambique and became an object of reverence. It was moved to Rachol Seminary (*see p71*) and a new image was installed here in 1836. The Fama of Menino Jesus is celebrated at the church in October.

6km (4 miles) west of Margao. Frequent buses from Margao stop near the popular Colva beachfront and in the village.

Damodar Temple at Zambaulim

Parvath

Shri Chandeshwar Bhutnath Temple
rises from a hill, offering a superb view
of the landscape. According to an
inscription, this pinnacle had a temple
from ancient times but the present
structure dates from about the 17th
century. The site is dedicated to
Chandeshwar, a manifestation of Lord
Shiva as the Moon God, and is laid out
to allow the moonlight to fall on the
deity. The subsidiary shrines or niches
to the rear of the main shrine house
images of Shiva's consort Parvati
to the west and his son Ganesh to
the east. A small shrine is dedicated
to Bhutnath.

Parvath (12km/7 miles southeast of
Margao on the main Quepem road).

Zambaulim

The **Damodar Temple** (*tel: 2602380*)
houses a lingam and idols rescued
from a temple pulled down by the
Portuguese in the 16th century. The
temple has been rebuilt and therefore
has a very modern appearance, but it
has a medieval tank beside the
Kushavati River that devotees believe
has medicinal properties.
Zambaulim is 22km (13½ miles)
southeast of Margao. Damodar
Temple is on the banks of the
Kushavati River.

SALCETTE

Salcette is one of the most fertile *talukas* of Goa, producing coconut, rice, cashews, fruits and vegetables. Away from its capital town, Margao (*see p66*), and situated inland from the coast, Salcette offers a glimpse of Goan village life and the chance to explore historic churches off the beaten track.

Chandor

This village has an interesting history as Chandrapur, the capital of the Kadamba Dynasty and a port on the once navigable Zuari River. Muslim and Christian rulers destroyed most of Chandor's historic past as a Hindu capital. The Sapta Matrika Temple was demolished in the 16th century and replaced by the **Church of Our Lady of Bethlehem** in 1645 (*tel: 2784002*).

Today, Chandor is best known for its Portuguese mansions, especially those near the Church Square. The **Menezes Braganza House** is one of the few Goan mansions that allow visitors to view the interior (*tel: 2784201. Open: 10am–5pm. Free admission but a donation is expected*).

This was the home of Luis de Menezes Braganza, a journalist and politician who from 1878 to 1938 campaigned for Goa's independence and for the benefit of the downtrodden. The house was built in the 16th century but was extended in the 18th and

The seminary at Rachol

19th centuries. It still contains carved rosewood furniture, porcelain tiles from Macau (dating from when Macau was a Portuguese enclave in China), Italian marble and mosaic floors.

The west wing has a restored teak ceiling over the library gallery, china and porcelain which display the family crest, and a ballroom with gilt mirrors, chandeliers and gold-leaf work on the doors. The east wing has furniture with the family initials, an Italian marble-topped table and a jumble of family relics. The main treasure in the family chapel is one of St Francis Xavier's nails.
About 13km (8 miles) east of Margao.

Curtorim

The **Church of St Alex** (*tel: 2786073*) was built in 1597, rebuilt in the 17th century and renovated in the 18th century. The interior is ornately decorated and has five altars, and the towers provide a good example of the Hindu influence on Goan church architecture.
9km (5¹/₂ miles) east of Margao.

Loutolim

Loutolim has many old Goan houses, including the Maendra Alvares family house which is open for public viewing. Alvares also developed the complex known as **Ancestral Goa**, which offers an insight into traditional Goa, and which has a number of re-created houses, ranging from a landowner's bungalow to a fisherman's shack and a farmer's home.

Tel: 2777034. www.ancestralgoa.com. Open: 9am–6pm. Admission charge. 10km (6 miles) northeast of Margao.

Rachol

A gateway and some walls are all that are left of the fort of Rachol, one of the most important early forts of Goa, which was built by the Muslims and captured in the 16th century by the Vijayanagara Dynasty. After repairs in 1745 by the Marquis, the fort was neglected and fell into decay.

The protection offered by the fort saw the establishment of one of Goa's most important seminaries at Rachol in 1580. Earlier called the College of All Saints, it was dedicated to Ignatius Loyola in 1622. The seminary suffered when the Portuguese repressed religious Orders, first in 1759 when the Jesuits were expelled and then in 1835 when the Oratorians who replaced them also lost favour, but it once more grew into a prestigious educational centre, and today it is a forward-looking institution with a college, hospital, school and an almost self-sufficient community.

Rachol also has a church dating from 1609 and renovated in 1622 with richly gilded interiors. The altar to St Constantine houses his relics and a statue of Menino Jesus, brought here from Colva.
The seminary is not open to visitors. Tel: 2777744. 7km (4¹/₂ miles) northeast of Margao. Frequent buses from Margao stop near the church.

Grand Goan houses

The stately houses of Goa are scattered across much of the state, but a large number are concentrated in the Salcette *taluka* along the South Goa coast. Most of the houses date from the 18th century when the Portuguese powers were at their zenith, with good income from their colonies in Africa and Latin America. These properties were integral to the status and lifestyle of the Goan aristocracy, which was granted large agricultural estates and land that it could rent out, powers in a feudal system, and the flow of income from expatriate earnings from Portugal and from Portuguese colonies.

This resulted in an interesting blend of architectural styles incorporating European influences and yet rooted in local tradition. The owners used local materials like soil, laterite for walls and pillars, indigenous hardwoods and bamboos, shell lime for mortaring, coconut palms for thatching, and terracotta tiles from Mangalore for roofing. However, they imported porcelain and silks from China, the Portuguese colony of Macau and southeast Asia, mirrors, chandeliers and glass from Europe, tapestries, mosaic and marble tiles, and some pieces of furniture from Portugal and Spain. Goa in the 18th century developed a superb furniture crafting industry under carpenters who drew from European designs and yet retained their traditional skills, ensuring that Goan furniture preserved its own peculiar features. Good examples of the expertise of the furniture crafters of the period can be seen in the churches and in those stately houses that have been opened for public viewing.

Some old Goan houses, like this one, can now be used to hold wedding receptions

The design of the stately houses developed its own style as well. Most houses had a Balcao or pillared portico where the family spent their summer evenings on stone benches, with a covered veranda running the length of the house. The classical façade of the stately house was decorated with mouldings and pilasters, and there were usually balconies with ornamental railings. Instead of glass, oyster-shell windows became a tradition in Goa, with shells cut into strips for framing the house windows.

After Goa was granted independence in 1961, the Indian government banned the landholding system and took over many of the estates from the aristocracy, who had until then continued a lavish lifestyle centred on their grand houses, financed by their high rent incomes even after the decline of the Portuguese empire. Some of these homes fell into neglect as the owners lost their source of income, but there are still houses that retain their grandeur and are worth seeing. The house of the Braganzas at Chandor (see p70) is open for viewing and is a museum of rosewood furniture, paintings and porcelain, besides offering visitors an opportunity to view its grand Portuguese façade and floors tiled with Italian marble and mosaic. Also at Chandor is the Fernandes House which has carved furniture and

The Braganza house at Chandor

is open to visitors (*tel: 2784245. Open: Mon–Sat 10am–5pm. Admission free but donations appreciated*). The Casa Araujo Alvares house opposite Ancestral Goa at Loutolim (*see p71*) is also worth a visit to see the wooden floors, chandeliers and mirrors from Europe, and its grand hall (*tel: 2777034. www. casaaraujoalvares.com. Admission charge*). Walking around Loutolim, see the façades of the Miranda house, Salvador Costa house and Roque Caetan Miranda house. Majorda, Colva and Madgaon also have impressive houses. In North Goa, Candolim, Calangute and Anjuna have impressive stately homes. The Piedade village on Divar Island also enjoys a good reputation for its attractive buildings.

THE SOUTH COAST

The south coast of Goa, comprising the *talukas* of Quepem and Canacona, has the hills of the Western Ghats and the coastline in close proximity to one another. Plateaux and wooded valleys lie along the coast, while forests such as the Cotigao Sanctuary are just 15km (9 miles) inland.

Beaches

Palolem is a beautiful beach, fringed by palms and known for its dolphin sightings. Its restaurants and shacks all enjoy a view of the coast, and the rocky outcrops on both sides of the curving stretch of sand are referred to locally as Pandawa's drums and footprints.

Agonda, to the north of Palolem, is a casuarina-lined beach that is growing in popularity.

Cabo de Rama Fort

This fort is named after Rama, hero of the Ramayana epic, who is said to have lived on this cape with his wife, Sita, and brother, Laxman. The fort existed on the headland for centuries, before the Portuguese conquered it in 1763 from the Raja of Sonda. It was practically rebuilt by the Portuguese but saw little action, except during the British occupation of Goa, and quietly fell into neglect.

Several cannons line the well-preserved ramparts, which offer superb views from the bastions. The church inside is still in use.

25km (15½ miles) south of Margao. Bus: buses leave from the Municipal Gardens in Margao from 7.30am. Admission free.

Canacona

The **Santa Tereza de Jesus Church** (*tel: 2644391*) was built in 1962 and lies south of Canacona town. **Shri Malikrjuna Temple**, northeast of town, is said to date from the 16th century and was renovated in 1778. It has a *mandapa*, or assembly hall, with carved wooden columns. In February, the festival of Shigmo attracts large crowds of devotees.

Canacona is 37km (23 miles) south of Margao en route from Panaji to Karnataka. Trains for Canacona leave from Margao, Mumbai, Panjim and Mangalore, and buses from Margao.

Partagali

Partagali is home to an important religious institution, **Shri Sanstan Gokarn Jeevotam Math**, established in Margao in 1475 and moved to Bhatkal in Karnataka during the Inquisition, before being established here. The huge banyan tree provides a place for quiet meditation, with a Shiva lingam in front, which is believed to have been a pilgrimage site for centuries. While it is still a religious establishment, the place has also developed into a centre for culture and learning.

45km (28 miles) south of Margao.

The palm-fringed beach at Palolem is populated by boats

Northern Goa

Much of the action for visitors to Goa goes on in the northern part of the state. In the 1960s, once sleepy fishing villages were co-opted into the tourist trail by visiting hippies, who were charmed by the picture perfect beaches and laid-back vibe, and these villages have been catering to the Western party crowd ever since. Meanwhile, the atmosphere of Goa-past remains in the form of forts, heritage hotels and picturesque inland villages.

BARDEZ

South of the River Chapora, the sweeping coastline of the *taluka* of Bardez has been a popular tourist spot for many years with its fine beaches, and enjoyable markets such as the 'Big Wednesday' flea market at Anjuna and the Friday bazaar at inland Mapusa (*see pp80–81*). Part of the Portuguese Old Conquest in Goa, Bardez has some of the best-preserved forts (*see pp78–9*) and churches in Goa.

Aldona

The **Church of St Thomas** (*tel: 2293352*) in the pretty village of Aldona dates from the late 16th century. It enjoys a great vantage point, overlooking the Mapusa River. Inside are imposing statues and several biblical murals. Several versions of a church legend exist, whereby thieves attempting to rob its treasures perished in the river.
Aldona is 4km (2½ miles) north of Pomburpa.

Beaches

Bardez has an almost continuous stretch of beach accessible from the resorts of Sinquerem, Candolim, Calangute, Baga, Anjuna and Vagator. Several hundred beach restaurants and 'shacks' line the coast from Sinquerem to Vagator. With varying degrees of crowds and facilities, selecting the ideal beach is largely a matter of personal choice.

Britona

The parish church of Britona, **Our Lady of the Rock of France**, has an excellent location at the meeting place of the Mandovi and the Mapusa rivers. The interior is beautifully decorated with painted scenes on the simple reredos. The church has been venerated as the protector of seamen since the 16th century, when a plague epidemic threatened a fleet of ships; the captain, with his crew, vowed that they would visit the church of Our Lady of the Rock of France in Lisbon if they survived.

About 5km (3 miles) away, at Pomburpa, is an impressive church, dedicated to **Our Lady Mother of God**, with rococo decorations. The interior of the church has elaborate panelling and stuccowork tracery.

Britona is 2km (1¼ miles) north of Panaji, off the Panaji–Mapusa stretch of National Highway 17 on the road running to Pomburpa along the Mapusa River.

Calangute

Away from the town centre of Calangute is the **Church of St Alex** (*Chagm Road. Tel: 2277378*). The current version of the church dates from the 18th century, and it provides a good example of the rococo decoration that became a feature of Goan Christian architecture in the 1700s. Noteworthy are the false dome of the façade, the gold and white schemes of the interior, the remarkable rococo pulpit and the fine reredos.

Calangute is 10.5km (6½ miles) northwest of Panaji. One of the busiest towns on the north coast of Goa, Calangute receives frequent buses from Mapusa and Panaji.

Colvale

Originally built in 1591, the **Church of St Francis of Assisi** (*tel: 2299867*) had (*Cont. on p82*)

Northern Goa

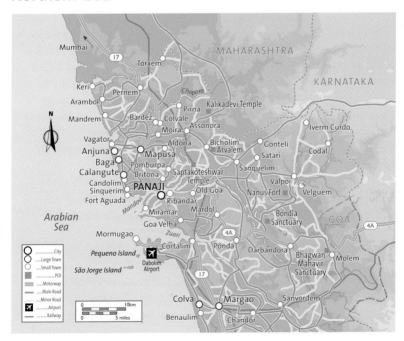

Tour: Forts of North Goa

Bardez and Pernem talukas have well-preserved forts, largely a legacy of Goa's attempts to protect itself against Dutch and Maratha incursions, and a tangible reminder of the presence and military might of the Portuguese. Some have survived the centuries better than others, but all evoke a sense of the state's chequered past.

Allow about 5 hours for this 65km (40-mile) tour.

Start at Panaji, turning left after Mandovi bridge and then hugging the coast to Reis Magos.

1 Reis Magos Fort

The military importance of the headland of Reis Magos was recognised by Afonso de Albuquerque who stationed forces here when he arrived at Goa. The fort was built here in the 1550s, but it lost some of its importance in the 17th century when Fort Aguada was built.

Just below the fort walls is the colourful Reis Magos Church, dedicated to the tale of the three Kings. It was built in 1555 and restored in the 18th century. The church interior is dominated by a painting on a wooden panel of the three gifts of gold, frankincense and myrrh to the infant Jesus.

The fort is not open to the public. Church: Tel: 0823 2402370. Open: Mon–Sat 9am–noon & 4.30–5.30pm. Free admission.

From Reis Magos, travel west to Nerul, passing Shantadurga Temple, then turn left for Fort Aguada.

2 Fort Aguada

One of the strongest of Goa's forts and among the best preserved, Fort Aguada is located on a headland that offered its architects an ideal location for defence. It also had the advantage of natural springs providing water to last through a siege. Today's visitors can enjoy the thick walls, the bastion on the hilltop and the old lighthouse.

Last admission around 4.30pm. Free admission.

From Fort Aguada, take the road north towards Anjuna. A couple of roads lead to Vagator, which then run into Chapora.

3 Chapora Fort

This fort stands on a rocky headland commanding the Chapora river estuary. Built in the 16th century by the Sultans, the fort was rebuilt by the Portuguese in the 17th century and again in 1717 to guard against threats of Maratha attacks. The fort fell to the Marathas in the same century and was taken again much later. After the Portuguese conquered the northern *taluka* of Pernem, the fort was no longer needed as a line of defence and was abandoned in the late 19th century. The fortifications contain Muslim tombs, ramparts and tunnels, and provide a panoramic sea view from the walls.

Open: 24 hours. Free admission.
Continue towards Mapusa.
After 2.5km (1½ miles) turn left to Siolim and then take the bridge across *the River Chapora. After the bridge, turn left and follow the coast. After Paliem, the road drops down to Keri for the ferry to Tiracol.*

4 Tiracol Fort

Tiracol is a tiny but strategically located fort. Built by the Bhosle Dynasty of Sawantwadi in the 17th century, it is protected from the sea and has moats along the landward-facing walls. The fort is now a heritage hotel (*tel: 02366 227631. www.forttiracol.com*). The Portuguese captured it in the 18th century and built **St Anthony's Church** inside.

Open to visitors for lunch and dinner.

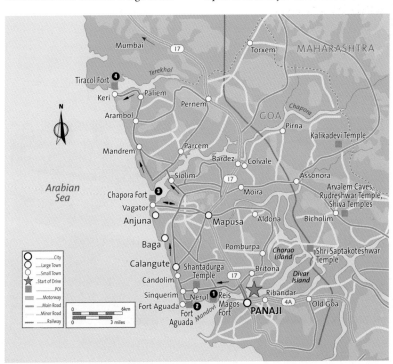

Bazaars and bargains

Anjuna

Anjuna's Wednesday Flea Market is famous and draws a large number of tourists. The market started as a place for long-staying western visitors, mainly hippies and backpackers, to sell belongings in order to be able to afford a longer stay at Anjuna Beach, and Indians used to come here in search of 'foreign goods' at bargain prices. From time to time the authorities have banned the market, for instance when it became a 'black market' for imported goods and the centre of an illicit narcotics trade.

Today, the market is more organised, with 'lots' rented out for stalls where Kashmiris, Tibetans, Nepalese, Rajasthanis and Gujaratis sell handicrafts and souvenirs. The most striking vendors are the colourfully dressed Lamanis from neighbouring Karnataka who come to sell tribal jewellery and traditional textiles fashioned into anything from clothes to bags. The market is convenient for travellers who can shop for beachwear, T-shirts, swimsuits, CDs, food, second-hand books and souvenirs. There are even stalls offering services such as hairdressing, henna-painting and tattooing. While early morning is good for serious shopping before the crowds arrive, the travellers' scene builds up in the afternoon.

A stall at Anjuna Market

Market Road, at southern end of beach. Open: Wed 8am–5pm or 6pm Oct–Mar/Apr.

Mapusa market

A market town for centuries, Mapusa is a good example of an Indian market, especially on Friday when it is very lively and colourful. Goans come here to shop for provisions such as fresh fish, vegetables, jackfruit, mangoes and plantain bananas, pickles and preserves, spices, bakery products and meats, particularly Goan sausages. There are shops and stalls selling household appliances, cooking utensils, clothes, fabrics, linen and jewellery fruits, while one lane is almost entirely dedicated to terracotta pottery. As the market has developed into a tourist attraction, Mapusa's Friday bazaar has also become a place for curios and souvenirs, and Lambadi women come here to sell trinkets, mirrored bags, purses and dress material.

Necklace vendor at Anjuna Market

Open: Sat–Thur 8am–6pm, Fri (the main market day) 8am–6.30pm.

Margao

Margao is well known for its covered market, southeast of the Municipal Gardens. The market is a good place for spices, fruit and flower garlands, as well as more practical purchases such as saris, clothes and kitchenware. Crowded and vibrant, a highlight of the market is stopping for a coconut juice: the fruit will be whipped into the necessary condition by the machete-wielding vendor. There's less to buy at the fish market, north of the town by the bus station, but it makes for an interesting wander if you're passing.
Open: Mon–Sat 8am–8pm.

Panaji

Panaji is not exactly a 'market hub' like Margao and Mapusa, but the municipal market is quite interesting for local colour and to see fresh fruits and the daily catch from the fishing boats.
Open: from 7.30am.

to be rebuilt in 1713 after being damaged during Maratha invasions. The façade has an impressive plaster image of St Francis between two angels. *Colvale is located 7km (4¼ miles) north of Mapusa on National Highway 17.*

Mapusa

Best known for its large market (*see p81*), Mapusa is also the site of **St Jerome's Church** (*tel: 2250590. www.stjeromesmapusa.com*), better known as Milagres Church. Built in 1594, it was rebuilt in the 17th century and restored after a fire in the 19th century. The church is small but attractive: inside are three retables (shelves) behind the altar which are among the most colourful in Goa. The main altar is to Our Lady of the Miracles, and there are side altars to St John and St Jerome.
Mapusa is 13km (8 miles) north of Panaji. It is the capital of Bardez taluka and is an important junction for buses.

The palm- and shack-lined coast along Vagator Beach

Moira

The **Church of Our Lady of the Immaculate Conception** (*tel: 2470555*) dominates the village of Moira. With its flat towers and false dome, the present version of the church was built in the 19th century to replace a mud-and-thatch church, and the bell was brought here from the Jesuit College of Monte Santo. An unusual art treasure is the crucifix, which has Jesus's feet nailed separately instead of together.
Approximately 5km (3 miles) east of Mapusa.

BICHOLIM AND SATARI

Bicholim and Satari are scenic areas of the North Goan interior, with lakes, waterfalls and the hills of the Western Ghats. They have been on the edges of political development, only becoming part of Goa after the New Conquests. Because of their remote locations, they became centres of refuge for Hindus escaping the Inquisition, and many temples sprang up here to house idols that were in danger of destruction in the Portuguese territory.

Arvalem

Arvalem has Buddhist caves cut into the rocks, which have recently been converted into Shiva temples. The caves are believed to date from the 1st to the 6th centuries, and the shrines where Buddhist images stood have been converted to house linga of Shiva. Near the caves are the Arvalem

Waterfalls, which are most impressive during the monsoon.
2km (1¹/₄ miles) northwest of Sanquelim, southeast of Bicholim.

Kansarpal

The century-old **Kalikadevi Temple** at Kansarpal has three silver-covered doors and an ornate door to the main shrine. The deity of the sanctum is Goddess Kali, and the layout is unusual in having two assembly halls leading to the main sanctuary.
At the northern end of Bicholim taluka.

Naroa

The tiny **Shri Saptakoteshwar Temple** is set in a beautiful forested area of Naroa (Narve). The temple is dedicated to Saptakoteshwar, an incarnation of Lord Shiva, who was the principal deity of the Kadamba Dynasty when it ruled over Goa, and who came to earth pleased with the meditation of the seven sages in his honour. The multifaceted lingam, which is the main image of the temple, was rescued from Divar Island, where the old temple was destroyed to make way for a church. It was reinstated at Naroa across the river from Divar during Shivaji's visit in 1668. Recently renovated, the temple has a lamp tower in the tradition of all Goan temples.
Approached from Divar Island by ferry.

Sanquelim

The **Datta Temple**, built in 1822, lies near the bazaar of Sanquelim, a village inhabited by the Ranes of Rajasthan. The temple is situated near the foot of a palm-covered hillock, and it is visited by devotees, who believe that Dattatrai's blessings cure insanity. The interior is white marble and the main shrine displays the *trimurti* (three-headed image) of Dattatrai.

Near the family home of the Ranes is the Vithal Temple. Built in the 14th century, this Vishnu Temple has been completely renovated, but some of the wooden columns are said to be original.
Regular buses between Mapusa and Valpoi stop at Sanquelim.

Satari

The main attraction of the Satari *taluka* is the unusual Brahma Temple at **Karmali**, a short drive out of town. The Brahma image, thought to date from the 11th century, was rescued from Carambolim near Old Goa and brought to this site where it was installed in the 16th century.
Karmali Temple is 9km (5¹/₂ miles) south of Valpoi, headquarters of Satari taluka.

Valpoi

This formerly sleepy village is now a lively and very attractive town, with churches, temples, a weekly market and occasional festivals. The main sight is **Nanus Fort**, the ruins of a 17th-century structure said to be one of the forts built by Shivaji, founder of the Maratha Empire. It was subsequently conquered by the Portuguese.
Valpoi is in the south of Satari.

Northern Karnataka

Bordering Goa but far less used to the patter of tourist feet, Northern Karnataka offers a convenient and laid-back excursion from India's smallest state. History buffs in particular will enjoy themselves, as this part of the country is home to some astonishing towns whose well preserved palaces and temples afford a tantalising glimpse of regal glories past. It is no slacker on the natural side either, with imposing coastal landscapes and attractive beaches all competing for your time.

HAMPI

The UNESCO World Heritage Site of Hampi represents the grandeur and architectural style of the great Vijayanagara Empire, regarded as the largest Hindu Empire of South India, in clusters of ruined monuments called the Royal Centre and the Sacred Centre, and in scores of temples and other buildings set among the hills and along the Tungabhadra River.

The sheer number of monuments spread over a large area, the fine architecture and intricate temple carvings, the atmosphere of devotion at the temples where Hindu rituals can be witnessed, and the fantastic, serene, almost magical atmosphere of the setting of lush plains and rocky hills strewn with towering boulders draw travellers to Hampi, many of them visitors from Goa who make a three- or four-day trip into Karnataka to see the architectural gems of the state.

Holy to Hindus for centuries, Hampi was selected as the site for Vijayanagar,

the City of Victory, by an amalgamation of Hindus fighting against the powerful Islamic invasions of the Deccan Plateau in the 14th century. While there are diverse opinions regarding the founding of the city, it is generally credited to Harihara and Bukka, two brothers in the service of the courts of Kapila and Anegondi on the north bank of the river, who established their independence by setting up Hampi as their kingdom after the devastation of Anegondi by the Islamic rulers.

The most glorious period of Hampi was during the reign of Krishnadevaraja who founded a powerful dynasty in the 16th century that saw the Vijayanagara Empire grow in power, wealth and extent. During his rule, Hampi was a major market for cotton, textiles, sugar, iron and spices, most of which were also major exports from his empire. Imports included silk from China, and Arab horses, which it is said was in agreement with the Portuguese powers of Goa who wanted to prevent the best horses from reaching the Islamic cavalry. The revenue accumulated from taxing trade and agriculture made the city enormously wealthy, described by European visitors as being larger than Rome, the best provided city in India, and the most powerful kingdom of India. Muslim envoys, such as Abdul Razak, were awestruck by the jewellery markets.

As can be seen even from the ruins of Hampi, the Vijayanagara rulers were patrons of art and architecture. They also worked towards the development of agriculture, textiles and new technologies, and developed an ingenious hydraulic system to channel water from the Tungabhadra River to tanks, fields and the city, including extensive waterworks such as a huge aqueduct.

Protected by the river and rocky ridges, and further fortified for protection, the artisans of Vijayanagar developed an architectural style that blended the buildings with the huge boulders and terrain around them, enhancing the beauty of the city. The city was destroyed after the defeat of the Vijayanagar army at the hands of a Muslim coalition of Sultans during the Battle of Talikota during 1564–5 and, without its powerful capital, the Vijayanagara Empire disintegrated.

Hampi is near Hospet, which receives trains from Vasco da Gama four times a week. The 283km (176 miles) journey takes $7^1/_2$ to $10^1/_2$ hours. Hospet has hotels and restaurants and, as Hampi has grown into a 'travellers' centre', there are eateries in the bazaar. A day pass can be bought for admission to the monuments at the Royal Enclave or at the Vithala Temple (see p90).

Northern Karnataka

Queen's Bath, Hampi

Anegondi and surrounds

The fortified town on the northern side of the river, Anegondi or Anegonda, predates Hampi and became a seat of power once more after the devastation of Vijaynagar city. The town retains some of its walls, gateways and watchtowers, traditional houses and temples. The **Huchchappayana Matha Temple** has carved panels of dancers, and the **Rangantha Temple** is still a living shrine. Some of the old palaces are in ruins, but the **Gagan Mahal Palace**, which now houses administrative offices, has graceful arches and pyramidal towers. The road west from Anegondi leads to a **Durga temple** and a **Hanuman temple**, perched on a rocky hilltop reached by a strenuous climb but rewarded by superb views of the monuments along the Tungabhadra River. A small track off this road leads to Pampasarovar,

Hemakuta Hill, Hampi

a bathing tank that is among the five lakes holy to Hindus, together with Mansarovar (now in Tibet), Pushkar in Rajasthan, Narayan Sarovar in Gujarat and the Bindusagar Tank at Bhubaneswar in Orissa. Visitors may get to witness ritual bathing at this lotus-covered body of water. Temples are generally open from dawn to dusk and free to enter.

Kamalapuram

The **archaeological museum** at Kamalapuram has a well-displayed collection of sculpture from local and surrounding sites, Neolithic tools, paintings, copper plates and coins. Gallery 1 is dedicated to Shaivite Hinduism with sculptures of Lord Shiva and his manifestations, Shakti's (goddesses denoting power, most of them Shiva's consorts) and Shiva's sons, Kartikeya and Ganesh, and a central hall in a typical temple layout with a Shivalinga and a Nandi (the bull of Lord Shiva). Gallery 2 is mainly dedicated to Vishnavite Hinduism and exhibits sculptures of Rangnath, Lakshmi Narayan (Lord Vishnu with his consort, goddess Lakshmi) and Sita, and fine relief carvings of Hanuman and Garuda. Gallery 3 has coins of the Vijayanagara Dynasty, arms and armoury, copper and brass plates and other antiquities. Gallery 4 has prehistoric and protohistoric finds. The museum has a scale model of Hampi in the courtyard and hero monuments stand in the gardens of the museum.

Lotus Mahal at the Royal Centre

*Archaeological Museum is five minutes'
walk from the bus station in
Kamalapuram. Tel: (08394) 241561.
Open: Sat–Thur 10am–5pm. Closed: Fri.
Admission charge.*

East of Kamalapuram is the
Pattabhirama Temple dedicated to
Lord Rama, and the remains of the old
walls of a suburban complex.
Continuing from Kamalapuram to
Talarighat, a path leads to a Muslim
enclave with a mosque, tomb and well.
*Kamalapuram lies within the Hampi
ruins, just outside the Royal Centre
(see below).*

Malyavanta Raghunatha Temple

Malyavanta Hill is associated with the
Ramayana. The 16th-century

Raghunatha Temple has Gopuram
gateways on the east and the south,
both with bands of relief carvings.
The main sanctuary is set around a
towering boulder carved with images of
Rama and Sita with Lakshamana and
Hanuman. A columned hall stands on
the south of the temple. Behind the
temple, natural crevices house lingas
and Nandis in relief.
*Islamic Quarter. Open: 6am–8pm.
Admission free.
On the road to Kampili, 6km (4 miles)
east of the Virupaksha Temple.*

Royal Centre

The structures enclosed by a huge
granite wall are generally thought to
comprise the royal enclave because of

The Elephant Stables at the Royal Centre

decorated platform to watch the pageantry and tournaments that were part of the festivities. Called the **Mahanavami Dibba**, or 'House of Victory', the pavilion is said to have been built to commemorate the successful efforts of Krishnadevaraja to contain the Gangas of Orissa who were a threat to the Vijayanagara Empire, and it has carvings on the platform portraying courtly scenes such as the king giving audiences, festivities and hunts. Other structures, such as the columned hall of audiences and the mint, are linked with the administration of the rulers.

The hydraulic engineering skills of the Vijayanagara rulers can be seen in the tanks, ducts, canals and sluices that carried water to different areas of the royal centre. An attractive stepped stone tank in the enclosure suggests the importance of the royal bath. The impressive **Queen's Bath** is housed in a rather plain building surrounded by a moat, with pretty stuccowork, projecting filigreed balconies and domes in different styles, and an excavated water supply channel can be seen outside.

The main religious building of the enclosure was **Hazara Rama Temple**, generally believed to have been the state shrine for the ruler. Though small, the temple is considered a fine example of Vijayanagara architecture and has vivid sculptures depicting episodes from the Ramayana along the walls. In the compound are two

the wealth that had to be protected by fortifications and the skilful courtly architecture associated with the residential area of rulers. The best representation of the courtly style of the Vijayanagara Dynasty, which drew from both Hindu and Islamic styles, is the 16th-century **Lotus Mahal**, screened by a wall because it was probably built for the queens, with cusped arches, bracketed windows and pyramidal domes. The **Elephant Stables** nearby have ten domed chambers with vaulted entrances representing different architectural styles, and beams to which elephants could be chained around a central pavilion, with a guardhouse at the entrance.

The main festival of Hampi was Mahanavami, and the rulers celebrated their rituals here and probably used the smaller temples in a similar style whose carvings show that they must have been dedicated to Narsimha and Lakshmi.

Near the Bhima Gate, a beautifully preserved arched gateway to the royal centre of Hampi, the 14th-century **Ganagitti Jain Temple** is crowned by a pyramidal tower.

Open: sunrise–sunset. Free admission (except for Lotus Mahal). Royal Centre, 3km (2 miles) south of Hampi Bazaar.

Sacred Centre

Set along the Tungabhadra River, the temples of the Sacred Centre are pre-Vijayanagara dynastic period, generally believed to date from the 9th to 11th centuries. The style of these temples usually comprises plain exteriors, stepped pyramidal towers and terraced galleries, and some of them crown rocky outcrops overlooking the ravines. They are best explored by walking from the Vithala Temple to the Virupaksha Temple (*see pp124–5*).

Hampi Bazaar.

Virupapur Gaddi

The other side of the river from Hampi, Virupapur Gaddi's remoteness appeals to some and deters others. Access is by coracle, a lightweight rowing boat, from the ghats north of Virupaksha Temple.

North of the Tungabhadra River.

The Virupaksha Temple is one of the most magnificent temples of Hampi

Walk: Hampi's Sacred Centre

This walk explores Hampi's sacred axis that runs from the Vithala Temple to the Virupaksha Temple, passing other temples, monuments and riverside sites.

Allow 3–4 hours for the walk, including time to see the significant temple sites.

Start at the Vithala Temple.

1 Vithala Temple

Vithala Temple is a UNESCO World Heritage Monument and is considered one of the finest examples of Vijayanagara period architecture. Believed to date from the 16th century, the temple is entered through Gopuram gatehouses. To the east of the temple is the famous Hampi chariot, a shrine designed like a wooden chariot on wheels, with fine carvings, including a depiction of Garuda, the eagle mount of Lord Vishnu. The open *mandapa*, or hallway, features intricate carvings at the front, while the superbly carved slender columns produced musical notes when struck. The ceiling is beautifully carved with floral and geometric patterns. The other columned halls also have interesting carvings.

Open: 8am–6pm. Admission charge.
Take the footpath at the rear of the temple.

0 —— 500 metres
0 —— 500 yards

N

Vithala Temple
1

King's Balance
2

Virupapur Gaddi

Tungabhadra River

Irrigation Channel

Virupaksha Temple
6

Hampi Bazaar

Nandi Statue

Kondanarama Temple

Achyutharajaya Temple
3

Achyutya Bazaar

Alternative return route

5

4

Krishna Temple

MATANGA HILL

★ ....Start of Walk
........POI

2 King's Balance

The rulers are said to have been weighed here against grain, gold or wealth for distribution among the poor. *Continuing from here, the path reaches the Kondanarama Temple from where a path turns left for Achyutharajaya Temple, passing through the Sule or Achyutya Bazaar, generally thought to have been a market for prostitutes.*

3 Achyutharajaya Temple

This temple has two Gopuram gatehouses leading to passageways inscribed with the names of donors. The columns within the main hallway are intricately carved with mythological and erotic scenes.
Open: sunrise–sunset. Free admission. Leave the Achyutharajaya Temple by the Gopuram to the right, and follow the path that leads past the Matanga Hill.

4 Nandi Statue

Beneath the boulders of the hill is a hall housing a colossal Nandi statue.
The path from here leads to granite steps descending to the Hampi Bazaar.

5 Hampi Bazaar

A long-ruined, colonnaded bazaar leading to a new market of shops, stalls and eateries mainly catering to travellers.
At the end of the market, the street runs to the eastern entrance of the Virupaksha Temple.

6 Virupaksha Temple

This temple is entered through two towering Gopuram gatehouses, one of

Detail of Vithala Temple

them more than 50m (164ft) high, leading to the courtyards. The temple predates the Vijayanagara period, showing Chalukyan and Hoysala architectural styles, but continued to be important during the reign of Krishnadevaraja who added Vijayanagara features to it, and it is still an important place of worship for Hindus. The colonnaded inner court leads to the main hall, with carved columns and ceiling, which is one of the few places in Hampi where the Vijayanagara style of painting can be seen. Dedicated to Virupaksha, an aspect of Lord Shiva, and his consort, the goddess Pampa, whose legend is associated with the Tungabhadra River, the temple attracts devout Hindus, particularly during festivals. Hampi's famous monolithic Narsimha statue, hewn out of a boulder, can be seen to the south of the temple.
Tel: (08394) 241241. Open: dawn–dusk. Admission charge.
End the walk at Virupaksha Temple or take the riverside footpath back from Hampi Bazaar to the Vithala Temple.

BIJAPUR

Bijapur has some of the most impressive Muslim monuments in southern India and is often billed the 'Agra of the South'. The town was once ruled by the Chalukya Dynasty and then by the Vijayanagara Empire before it was conquered by the Sultans of Delhi. After a period of Brahmani Sultan rule, the governor of Bijapur, Yusuf Adil Shah, won independence from Bidar and made Bijapur his capital in the 15th century.

The building boom of Bijapur came after the five Muslim dynasties united against the Vijayanagara forces in 1564–5. The wealth that resulted from the rout of Vijayanagar (Hampi) brought about the golden period of Indo-Islamic architecture of Bijapur, which lasted for more than a century.

However, disputes between the sultans and within the Adil Shahi Dynasty resurfaced, and the Bijapur Sultanate fell into decay by the late 17th century when the Mughals took over.

Bijapur still retains its air of a medieval Muslim citadel with its mosques, mausoleum complexes and palaces that reflect both the Turkish origin of the Sultans and the regional influences of the Hindu majority of Karnataka.

Bijapur is accessible by bus from Hospet and by train from Mumbai and Pune. Most visitors drive to Bijapur following National Highway 13 from Hampi (see pp84–91). It has hotels and restaurants, most of them located on Station Road.

For more information on the sights, visit the Tourist Office, Station Road. Tel: (08352) 250359. Open: Mon–Sat 10am–5.30pm.

The citadel

The citadel stands in the heart of town with much of its old wall and moat still extant. It houses the Gangan Mahal, or 'Heavenly Palace', of Ali Adil Shah, and its platform served as the hall of audiences, facing the crowds. The Mecca Masjid, a small mosque in the citadel, is believed to have been built for women. The Mehtar Mahal, the 'Sweeper's Palace', is ornamented with relief work on balconies and ceilings. The Anand Mahal was built by Ibrahim, and nearby is the Taj Baori, a stepped tank and a women's quarter, named after his wife. Sat Manzil was a pleasure palace of a courtesan, and Jal Mandir was a water pavilion. Many other buildings are now government offices.

North of the citadel is the Bara Kaman or 12 archways, a mausoleum for Ali Rauza built in the 17th century but left incomplete after his death. Set on a plinth, the columns connected by arches surround the tomb in the courtyard.

Golgumbaz

Bijapur's largest and most celebrated monument, the Golgumbaz was built as a mausoleum of Muhammad Adil Shah in the 17th century. The mausoleum is noted for its dome, which is one of the largest unsupported domes in the world, and is only a little smaller than the one crowning St Peter's in Rome. It rises among attractively landscaped gardens, and the gatehouse in front of the building is a museum that houses sculpture, paintings depicting the Sultans and Begums of Bijapur, miniatures of courtly scenes, battles and hunts, weapons, porcelain, parchments, the famous bidriware, or metalwork, of the Deccan, carpets, coins and other relics of Bijapur's glorious medieval past.

The mausoleum building is buttressed by seven-storey octagonal towers surmounted by small domes.

Inside is the hall that is considered the largest in the world covered by a single hemispherical dome, about 170sq m (1,830sq ft) in area with a plinth on which are located the tombs of Muhammad Adil Shah, his wife and others dear to him. Spiralling staircases run up to the Whispering Gallery, a passage circling the dome, which gives a feel of the size of the building. The gallery is known for its acoustics that are said to enable even the most hushed whisper to echo across the passage.

The spectacular dome is the most prominent feature of Golgumbaz

2km (1¹/₄ miles) east of the city centre.
Monument open: 6am–5.40pm.
Museum open: Sat–Thur 10am–5pm.
Separate admission charges for the
monument and the museum.

Ibrahim Rauza

This mausoleum is one of the
highlights of Bijapuri architecture.
Built by Ibrahim II, who came to the
throne in the 1580s, and his wife Taj
Sultana, the mausoleum has minarets,
cupolas, stone filigree and sculptural
work that are said to have inspired the
Taj Mahal. The mosque and the
mausoleum are set on two sides of a
plinth that has a water tank and
fountains. The walls have elaborate
Koranic inscriptions that rank among
the best in India, latticed windows,
decorative panels and beautiful stone
sculptures, including a chain carved
from a single stone. It is a testimony to
a period when arts and crafts thrived
in Bijapur under the rule of Ibrahim II.
Open: 6am–6pm. Admission charge.
South of MG Road, to the west end of
the town.

Jama Masjid was built in the 16th century

The giant Malik-i-Maidan cannon

Jama Masjid

The Jama Masjid, or Jumi Masjid, is one of the finest of the 16th-century mosques of the Deccan, superbly proportioned and topped by onion domes. The mosque was built by Ali Adil Shah, who is credited with building the fortifications of Bijapur and excavating the extensive waterworks soon after the successful battle with Vijayanagara rulers. The mosque has an arcaded court with a square tank leading to the main prayer hall with its elegant central dome surrounded by 33 smaller domes. The grand entrance to the prayer hall was added by Mughal emperor Aurangzeb, and it has rectangular markings for about 2,500 worshippers to pray, although there could be twice that number during the Friday Namaz. The *mihrab* (prayer niche) is richly embellished with goldwork, calligraphy and floral decorations.

Open: 9am–5.30pm. Free admission.
1km (²/₃ mile) southwest of Golgumbaz.

Malik-i-Maidan

On a bastion with ornamental stone lions called Burj-i-Shera ('Lion Bastion'), the Malik-i-Maidan, or Lord of the Plains, is one of the world's largest cannons. Brought to Bijapur as war booty, the cannon, cast in the 16th century, weighs about 55 tons. After winning the battle against the Ahmednagar Sultans, the Bijapur army brought the cannon here using 10 elephants, 400 bullocks and a large battalion of men. The muzzle of the cannon is shaped like the mouth of a monstrous lion devouring an elephant. The surface is dark green and polished, and touching it is supposed to bring good luck.

North of MG Road by the citadel.

Upli Buruj

This 16th-century watchtower affords excellent views of the surrounding area. At the top of the 24m (79ft) structure are two large cannons.

At the western end of the citadel.

BADAMI

Badami has some of the finest examples of rock-cut cave and early temple architecture in southern India. The capital of the Chalukya Dynasty, whose empire covered much of the Deccan Plateau from Gujarat to Tamil Nadu in the 6th and 7th centuries, Badami is set in a gorge among sandstone ridges.

Badami is off National Highway 13, which leads from Hampi to Bijapur. Buses take 3 hours to Badami from Hubli, which is connected by train to Vasco da Gama in Goa. Badami has hotels and restaurants.

Cave temples

The most visited monuments of Badami, the four cave temples carved into the hills in the 6th century, are largely Hindu, with the exception of a Jain temple. Although these rock-cut caves are modest in size and plan, they give the appearance of richness because of the delicately carved jewellery worn by the deities, the fine sculptural work of the smaller figures and the decorative ceilings.

The complex is open from sunrise to sunset. The admission charge covers the four caves. English-speaking guides are often available at the complex. Monkeys can be a nuisance, especially if you are carrying any food.
About 40 steps lead to the first cave, which has flights of steps connecting it to the other three caves in succession.

Cave 1

This is a Shiva temple and is probably the earliest of the four caves. It has several sculpted figures, such as Shiva's dwarf attendants on the plinth, a temple door-guard beside a Nandi bull, a striking image of a 16-armed Natraj manifestation of Shiva in 81 dancing poses, Harihara, which is the blend between Vishnu and Shiva with their respective consorts Lakshmi and Parvati and both their mounts, Garuda and Nandi, Ardhanarishvara, which is the part-male and part-female version of Shiva combined with Parvati, and ceiling panels depicting Lord Shiva and goddess Parvati, the serpent Naga and flying couples.

Cave 2

This is a Vishnu cave temple with relief carvings of Vishnu avatars ('incarnations') such as the boar Varah, the dwarf Vamana or Trivikama, a snake couple, and ceiling carvings depicting Vishnu riding the eagle Garuda, swastikas and Vishnu's Matsya, or 'fish', avatar.

Cave 3

This is generally considered to be the most impressive of the four cave temples because of its elaborate sculptural decoration and sheer size. The cave has striking depictions of couples as carved brackets, Lord Vishnu on the coils of the serpent Anantha and Vishnu's incarnations such as Narsimha, the man-lion combination that disembowelled a demon, and Varah or the boar incarnation. The cave has sculpted columns and fine images of Indra on an elephant, Shiva on a bull and Brahma riding a swan on the ceiling panels. Inscriptions date the cave to AD 578.

Cave 4

This cave, carved in the 7th and 8th centuries, is a Jain shrine to Adinatha, the first *tirthankar* (*see p16*), and has images of the 24 *tirthankars* lining the walls.

The temples

The area to the north of Agastya Lake has a number of 7th-century temples such as the rock-perched Mallegetti Shivalaya Temple, which is rated as one of the finest examples of early Southern Indian architecture. The Upper Shivalaya Temple is one of the oldest temples near the North Fort area and, although it is largely ruined, there are some interesting friezes depicting episodes from the tale of Lord Krishna.

Northern Karnataka

The entrance to the caves

AIHOLE

Generally referred to as the cradle of temple architecture, Aihole has more than 100 temples built in different styles such as the early Chalukyan, late Chalukyan, Hoysala, Nagara and Dravidian. This was the first capital of the Chalukyan Empire, evidence of its wealth and importance is seen in the remains of an ancient wall and its gates, which are among the earliest examples of such heavy fortifications found in this part of India.

Some of the temples were used as houses or cattle sheds, bearing today the names of their owners, and they are still remarkably well preserved.

Aihole is a day's excursion from Badami and is located off National Highway 13. It is often visited when travelling between Hampi and Badami. Aihole has places to stay and eat.

The most important temples, such as the **Durga Temple** and **Lad Khan Temple**, are grouped in a park, with an **archaeological museum** near the Durga Temple exhibiting fine examples of Chalukyan-period sculpture (*tel: 08351 284551. Open: Sat–Thur 10am–5pm*). There is an admission charge that covers the temples and museum in the park.

Durgigudi (Durga) Temple

One of the most important temples of Aihole, Durgigudi is named after its location near the Durg (Fort) walls.

It is notable for its early Gopuram-style entrance structure, Buddhist-style semicircular apse, elevated plinth featuring panels of intricate carvings, and the gallery around the sanctum that has a series of elaborate sculpture in niches, such as Lord Shiva with Nandi, Narasimha, Lord Vishnu with Garuda, Varaha, or the boar incarnation of Lord Vishnu, Durga, or Chamundi, destroying the buffalo-headed demon Mahisura, and Harihara, the combination of Vishnu and Shiva. Amorous couples are sculpted on the columns, and the entrance doorway to the hall has outstandingly rich sculpture. *Tel: 08351 284533. Open: 8am–6pm. Admission charge.*

Gaudar Gudi Temple

This small temple has a rectangular columned hallway surrounded by a gallery for walking around, and a roof in northern Indian style. Near this is a small temple with a frieze of ports and a well.

The Kunti group

The four Kunti temples form a rough square. Their notable features are the sculptures of amorous couples on the columns, and the ceiling panels of Shiva with Parvati, Vishnu and Brahma.

Lad Khan Temple

This temple is believed to have been used for royal weddings and assemblies.

A rectangular porch leads to the square plan of the interior, and the columns are richly carved. The temple has a Nandi and a shrine with a lingam near the rear wall, which may have been later additions. The temple gets its name from Lad Khan who was a Muslim noble residing here.

Open: 6am–6pm. Admission charge.

Meguti Temple

This hilltop temple is one of the earliest structures in Aihole, dated to AD 634 by an inscription. It is in Dravidian style with a lavishly decorated interior. The porch leads to a hallway and an upper storey above the sanctuary with a good view and an impressive Jain image in the sanctum.

Ravanphadi Temple

This rock-cut cave temple, excavated in the 6th century, has a Shiva shrine. Sculptural highlights include Ardhanarishvara, or part-male and part-female aspect of Shiva, Nateshan (a Shiva manifestation) dancing with Parvati, Ganesh, the Sapta Matrikas ('Seven Mothers'), and a huge lotus.

Lad Khan Temple was used for official ceremonies

PATTADAKAL

A UNESCO World Heritage Site, the riverside village of Pattadakal has the most mature examples of Western Chalukya architecture. Once the site of coronation ceremonies of the Chalukyan rulers, Pattadakal has temples dating from the 3rd century to the 7th century that are considered to be the climax of Western Chalukya architecture, and some that were built by the Rashtrakutas after they took over the kingdom from the Chalukya Dynasty.

Pattadakal was important in the development of South Indian architecture. While most of the temples are in the Dravidian style, a few are in the North Indian Nagara style, illustrating the region's position at the crossroads of Dravidian and Aryan traditions of South and North India respectively.

Two kinds of temple roofs can be seen in the same group of temples –

Detail of one of the walls of Virupaksha Temple

curvilinear towers and the square roofs with receding towers.

Built from the local sandstone, the temples are generally clustered at the foot of hills, and the most important group is in the compound of the archaeological park. Most of them are Shiva temples.

Pattadakal is about 20km (12¹/₂ miles) east of Badami and can be visited when travelling from Hampi to Badami.
The important temples are clustered in an archaeological park (tel: 08357 243118. Open: 6am–6pm. Admission charge).

Jambulinga Temple

The largely ruined 8th-century Jambulinga Temple near the entrance of the archaeological compound has temple guardians carved at the gateway, an image of Shiva and Parvati, and a good example of the curvilinear towers of the region. The Kadasiddheshvara Temple nearby is similar.

Mallikarjuna and Virupaksha temples

This pair of similar-looking temples is the largest in the group and must have been among the most elaborate temples in this part of India in the 8th century. Built by two sisters, who were queens of the Chalukyan ruler, Vikramaditya, the temples are said to have commemorated the conquest of Kanchipuram by the Chalukyas. Typifying the Dravidian tradition in their architectural details, the temples have richly carved three-storey towers with striking panels showing different forms of Shiva and Vishnu, and a carved base. Like most South Indian temples, the interiors are also exquisitely carved, with the pillars of the Virupaksha Temple relating tales from the Ramayana and Mahabharata epics, and those of the Mallikarjuna Temple carved with scenes from Krishna stories in delicately executed relief. Carvings in the temples also reflect the courtly and social life of the Chalukyas. A large chlorite Nandi stands in a pavilion facing the Virupaksha Temple, which has a black lingam in the sanctum.

Papanath Temple

This is one of the major temples at Pattadakal that shows the influences of the Nagara or northern style of architecture. The temple is surmounted by a shikhara, or curved temple tower, that would not look out of place in Orissa further north, and the exteriors are carved with episodes from the Ramayana in relief. Two columned hallways precede the sanctum with an open porch for the congregation.

Sangameshwar Temple

The earliest temple in the group, Sangameshwar was built during the reign of Vijaydabhya (AD 696–733). It is a perfectly proportioned temple with mouldings on the basement and pilasters dividing the wall, a corridor around the sanctum with the lingam and a multi-storey tower.

KARAVALI COAST

The coastal route from Goa to Kerala along the south Konkan or Karavali region, followed by the National Highway 17 and the Konkan Railway, is one of the most scenic in India. It runs between the Western Ghats and the Arabian Sea, offering views of both the lush greenery of the wettest sections of the South Indian hills and the serene sea called the 'Sapphire Coast', with some good beaches near Gokarna town and Mangalore city.

Gokarna

Gokarna is rapidly becoming popular as a beach resort for those who want to get away from the crowds of Goa. The famous Om Beach is named after its curving stretch of sand in the shape of the Hindu *Om*, while Kudle, Half Moon and Paradise beaches are also gaining popularity.

Gokarna is also one of the sacred sites of the southwest coast of India. The town has one of the most famous lingas on the west coast of India, housed in the Shri Mahabaleshvara Temple. The lingam is called the *Mahabala* ('the strong one'), *Atmalinga* or *pranalinga*, considered particularly powerful because of a local legend according to which it came to rest here after being carried off from Shiva's abode, Mount Kailash, by the demon king Ravana. The tale goes that Ganesh tricked Ravana by assuring him that he would look after the lingam while the latter prayed, knowing that it would take root once kept on the ground. As Ravana could not lift the lingam again it is said to have rested here since. Considered a powerful lingam so auspicious that a *darshan* ('vision') cleanses the devotee of all sins, it attracts Hindu pilgrims. As bathing is essential in Hinduism before prayer, pilgrims usually begin with a dip in the sea and take a ritual bath at the nearby stream, which is also considered holy for immersing ashes, before visiting the Shri Mahabaleshvara Temple. They also visit Ganesh's temple, Shri Mahaganpati Mandir, nearby.

Gokarna is on the main Konkan Railway line from Goa to Cochin 50km (31 miles) south of Karwar. The town has hotels and restaurants, as well as a few incipient beachside resorts nearby. Some of the temples are not open for non-Hindus, but rituals can be witnessed from outside.

Karwar

Karwar has a naval port and is surrounded by islands like Anjedive where men from Vasco da Gama's ship are believed to have found a ruined temple and water tank. Franciscan missionaries visited the island in 1500 and made their first converts on Indian soil at Anjedive. The Portuguese fort, built in 1505, was abandoned and then occupied in the 17th century by the British, whose tombs can still be seen. The Portuguese rebuilt the fort and cannons were added in 1731.

Karwar is on the main Konkan Railway line from Goa to Cochin 230km (143 miles) north of Mangalore. There are a few hotels in the town. Karwar is also the base from which to visit Devbagh Island and Jog Falls (see pp136–7).

Mangalore

Sandwiched between one of the wettest stretches of the Western Ghats and the coastline, Mangalore is a pleasant break from Goa. This idyllic location, between the spice- and cashew-rich hills and the coast, made Mangalore an important trading post in medieval times. Known for its pepper, Mangalore, or Manjuran, grew to become a vital port city in the 14th and 15th centuries when it was visited by merchants from Arabia and the Persian Gulf. Ibn Batutta in 1314, Razzak in the 1400s and Duarte Barbosa in 1514 noted that Mangalore lies in a land rich in rice and spices, exporting to the Middle Eastern and Mediterranean countries, and visited by overseas traders in large numbers. As tales of the port's riches spread, the Nayaka princes of Mangalore found their seat of power coveted by foreign powers. The Portuguese succeeded in conquering Mangalore in the 16th century, and set up factories here in the 17th and 18th centuries. The Sultans of Mysore laid siege to the place in the 19th century, and it was ruled for some time by Tipu Sultan who set it up as a shipbuilding centre.

Fishermen on the beach at Gokarna

Finally, the British took Mangalore, and it remained a colony of the Raj until India's independence in 1947. The city has developed into one of the ten most important ports of India and is a significant centre for the cashew trade.

One of the highlights of Mangalore is **St Aloysius Chapel**, built in 1885 on Lighthouse Hill (*Lighthouse Hill Road. www.staloysius.ac.in. Open: Mon–Sat 8.30am–6pm, Sun 10am–noon & 2–6pm. Free admission*). The chapel's interiors are painted with a variety of scenes by Italian priest Moscheni, in the fresco technique popularised by the famous artist Michelangelo. The chapel is now part of the St Aloysius college campus, which has an interesting museum that started as a research and reference centre for biology students, with stuffed animals, anatomy and other exhibits, and is now open to the public. Besides the natural history and other biological exhibits, the museum has a set of utensils and household implements used by Mangalorean families, along with a number of other exhibits that offer an insight into life in Mangalore in the 1930s and 1940s. A 1906 De Dion Bouton, donated to the college by Saldhana, a coffee curing tycoon of Karnataka, and exhibited in the museum, was one of the first cars to come to Mangalore.

Mangalore also has Hindu temples such as the **Shri Manjunath Mandir**, one of the oldest temples in the town and an important centre of Shivaite pilgrimage (*Kadri. Tel: (0824) 2214176.*

Open: 6am–1pm & 4–8pm. Free admission). The temple has a fine collection of bronze sculpture (the 10th-century Lokeshwara bronze is rated among the finest in Karnataka) and images. The temple is in the Kerala style, with a tiled roof and pagoda-like shape, but recent renovations unfortunately intrude on the original architecture of the temple. The temple grounds have nine water tanks, subsidiary shrines and a hermitage. A cave cut into rocks is associated with the Pandavas. The temple is an important centre for the tantric Natha-Pantha cult, which has a monastery here.

Another important temple is the **Mangaladevi Temple**, dating from the 10th century, and named after Mangala Devi, a princess from Mangalore. It has traditional Mangalore tiled roofing (*Bolar. Tel: (0824) 2425476*).

The **Shreemanthi Bai Memorial Government Museum** has an interesting collection of 15th- to 18th-century bronzes, 13th- and 16th-century stone sculpture, a 17th-century Nepalese statue, and some ethnology exhibits, woodcarvings, paintings and porcelain (*tel: (0824) 2211106. Open: Tue–Sun 9am–5pm. Closed: Mon. Admission charge. Bus: 19*).

The **Mahatma Gandhi Museum** in Canara School has a collection of sculpture, art, coins and stuffed animals (*Canara School. Tel: (0824) 2493210. Open: Mon–Sat 9.30am–12.30pm & 2–5.30pm. Closed: Sun and holidays. Free admission*).

Ceremonial cast at the Krishna Temple, Udupi

357km (222 miles) west of Bangalore.
The city has good hotels and there is a
beach resort at Ulal about 10km
(6 miles) away.

Udupi

Udupi is one of the most important
Vaishnavite centres on the southwest coast
of India. It is the birthplace of Madhva,
a saint who set up monasteries in the
town in the 13th and 14th centuries.

The centre of religious activity is
the **Krishna Temple**, set around a large
tank called the Madhva Sarovara that
devotees believe has associations with
the holy River Ganges. The idol in the
temple is believed by devotees to have
been found by Madhva, who, according
to local folk tales, prevented a
shipwreck and, when asked by the
captain to choose from the riches on

the vessel, took a block that exposed a
Krishna idol. Another local legend
holds that the idol of Lord Krishna
turned around to give *darshan* to a
devotee from a lower caste who was
not allowed access to the shrine
(*Car Street. Tel: (0820) 2520598.*
Open: 3.30am–10pm. Free admission).

Another important pilgrimage is to
Shri Ananthasana Temple, which is
associated with Madhva.

A short drive from Udupi is the
fishing port of **Malpe**. It is associated
with Vasco da Gama who is said to have
landed at St Mary's Isle and set up a
cross before his historic landing at
Kappad in Kerala.

Udupi is on the main Konkan Railway
line from Goa to Cochin, 58km
(36 miles) north of Mangalore. There are
a few places to stay and eat there.

Southern Maharashtra

The main point of interest in Southern Maharashtra – and a typical arrival point for travellers flying into the region – is Mumbai. A vivid urban Indian agglomeration teeming with people (some 14 million of them), the city is India's economic and cultural capital. Outside of the city, highlights of the region include the scenic Konkan Coast, skirted by the famous railway of the same name, and a few historical towns of note.

MUMBAI (BOMBAY)

Mumbai is the principal gateway to the west coast of India, including Goa, for most international travellers. The economic powerhouse of India and one of the country's most westernised cities, Mumbai's tremendous drive overcomes problems like overpopulation, traffic congestion, the filth and poverty of the city's slums and fumes to make it the capital of Indian industry, trade, stock exchange, fashion and film-making.

Sprawling Mumbai might at times be bewildering in its size and hectic pace of life, but this is just part of what makes it such an intoxicating and compelling city. India's beating economic and cultural heart has less of a hard edge than the actual capital of Delhi, which makes it an easy place to warm to, despite its enormity. It is a tribute to Mumbai's huge spirit that the city bounced back so resolutely from the devastating terrorist attacks of 2008. While the consequences of that night are evident in the thick layer of

security that now envelopes venues from the top hotels, civic and political centres to the lowliest internet cafe, tourists have not abandoned the city, and daily life here continues with all the verve and optimism of before.

Much of Mumbai's grandeur comes from its buildings, many of which bear the hallmarks of Britain's control of the city, under its anglicised moniker, Bombay. The European visitor cannot help but feel at home among the neat parks and English-style attractions. That said, Mumbai is still unmistakably Indian, with exotic smells and sounds that bewitch the foreign traveller. Though it has a wealth of individual landmarks, much of the pleasure comes from simply walking its heaving streets and imbibing the atmosphere.

Made up of seven islands, Mumbai is a vast city. The areas of most interest to visitors are largely found around the two main railway termini, Churchgate and CST (Chhatrapati Shivaji Terminus). Colaba is the drinking and

The area of Colaba

shopping hub, while nearby Fort is fairly self-explanatory. Nariman Point is another popular stop on the tourist trail, while upmarket Malabar Hill and the northern suburbs also have their plush attractions. The city can be navigated by taxi and auto-rickshaw, but the long distances involved can often lead visitors to the train system – which, with its often packed services that sometimes stop at the station for a matter of seconds, can be a travel experience in itself.

The Fort

The Fort area has most of the British era's earliest and most impressive buildings in Mumbai, erected during the building boom in the 1870s and again in the first two decades of the 20th century when King George V visited Mumbai, first as the Prince of Wales in 1905 and then as the reigning monarch in 1911. Following the Backbay reclamation projects of the 1920s, the Fort and Colaba areas saw the creation of apartment buildings and cinema halls in the Art Deco style.

Chhatrapati Shivaji Maharaj Vastu Sanghralaya (formerly Prince of Wales Museum)

This museum is housed in a building founded to commemorate the visit of the Prince of Wales in 1905, and it was opened only during 1922–3. Designed by architect George Wittet, it is an impressive museum building blending Victorian Gothic and Indo-Islamic features. The museum has some wonderful collections; after the key gallery introduces the visitor to the

Chhatrapati Shivaji Maharaj Vastu Sanghralaya

Dome of Victoria Terminus at dusk

highlights, the museum divides into archaeological, art and natural history sections. The archaeological section has pre- and protohistoric finds, mainly from Harappan excavations, and fine examples of Brahmanical, Buddhist and Jain sculpture, including Gadharan Buddhas of the 4th and 5th centuries, 7th-century Chalukyan panels from Aihole, and Gupta-period Buddhist stuccos. The art section has a collection of Indian paintings, including illustrated manuscripts and miniatures from the Mughal court, miniatures from the Mewar princely state and the Deogarh thikana, devotional pichwai paintings from Nathdwara and Deccani paintings. The museum also has Chola bronzes, Gujarati woodcarving, textiles, and decorative arts in jade, wood, ivory,

metal and silver. The Buddhist art collection depicts tantric Buddhism through sculpture of deities and the early founders of Tibetan Buddhism, thangka paintings and ritual objects. International collections include European paintings and ceramics, and glassware, printed fabrics and arts from China and Japan. The natural history section mainly exhibits stuffed mammals, birds and reptiles in dioramas re-creating their natural environment. The museum has been undergoing modernisation and reorganisation to give it a more interactive side, which is expected to be completed by the end of 2010.
159–161 Mahatma Gandhi Road.
Tel: (022) 22844519.
Email: crescent@giasbm01.vsnl.net.in.
www.bombaymuseum.org.
Open: Tue–Sun 10.15am–5.45pm.
Closed: Mon. Admission charge.

Chhatrapati Shivaji Terminus (Victoria Terminus)

This remarkable and elaborate example of Indo-Gothic architecture in Mumbai, also called the 'VT Station' by the people of Mumbai, was opened in 1887 to celebrate the golden jubilee year of Queen Victoria, more than three decades after the first train ran from this terminus to Thane. The building, designed by S W Stevens, has a huge central dome surmounted by a statue that was executed by the Bombay School of Art – *Progress* by Thomas Earp – Corinthian columns,

spires and minarets. The ticket hall, inspired by St Pancras Station in London, has stained glass, glazed tiles and arches. Since the attack on the station in 2008 there is now a visible security presence and metal detectors.
Dr. D Naoroji Road, Nagar Chowk.
Tel: (022) 2265 6565. Open: the train network runs from around 4–1am.
Free admission.

National Gallery of Modern Art (NGMA)

Now open for over half a century, the gallery also has outlets in New Delhi and Bangalore. The 14,000 total exhibits include both native and foreign artists and sculptors. One of the biggest names to go on show here is Pablo Picasso. There are also some Egyptian artefacts on display. The gallery is housed in the Sir Cowasji Jehangir Public Hall, a modern and professional venue suited to the theme.
Opposite Prince of Wales Museum.
Tel: (022) 22881971.
Email: ngma_mumbai@vsnl.net.
www.ngmaindia.gov.in.
Open: Tue–Sun 11am–7pm.
Closed: Mon.

The Oval

The green ground called the Oval Maidan is surrounded by imposing Victorian civil buildings and Art Deco apartment blocks. The 1857 Mumbai University campus is here and features buildings designed by Gilbert Scott,

Elphinstone College near the Oval

famous for the Gothic architecture of St Pancras Station in London. The university's convocation hall has often been compared to 15th-century Italian and French buildings, and the Rajabhai Clock Tower, standing 79m (259ft) high, is said to be based on Giotto's campanile in Florence. The neighbouring High Court has a high central tower flanked by lower octagonal towers with figures of Justice and Mercy. The Old Secretariat, which now serves as a civil and sessions court, the Public Works Office and Elphinstone College are other good examples of Victorian-period architecture near the Oval.

South of Churchgate Station, to the west of High Court and University.

South and central Mumbai

While most heritage tours and walks in Mumbai focus on the Fort area, there is much to be seen of historic, religious and architectural importance in areas like Colaba, in the markets and in Byculla and Mahalaxmi.

Byculla

Bhau Daji Lad Museum (Victoria & Albert Museum) Inspired by London's V&A, this museum was built in Palladian style in the 19th century. The galleries of the recently restored museum have ornamental walls, ceilings, railings and columns. The original curator of the museum was physician Sir George Birdwood, author of *The Industrial Arts of India* and an

(*Cont. on p114*)

Walk: Colonial Mumbai

Connecting two landmarks that define the landscape of Mumbai (Bombay), the Gateway of India and the Chhatrapati Shivaji Terminus, this recommended walking route through the Colaba and Fort areas of Mumbai visits the sites of some of the earliest British-era constructions in the city.

Allow 4 hours for the walk, including time to see the museums, art galleries and buildings on the route.

Start at Apollo Bunder.

1 The Gateway of India

Commemorating the visit of King George V in 1911, accompanied by Queen Mary, when they stepped ashore at Apollo Bunder, this monumental gateway facing the harbour was completed during 1923–4 by architect George Wittet. Wittet built many of Mumbai's great buildings in an eclectic style, incorporating the Indo-Saracenic style of blending Hindu and Islamic architecture that developed in Gujarat in the 15th and 16th centuries, the imposing Deccani Islamic architecture of Bijapur and Victorian Gothic features. The honey-coloured basalt gateway, comprising a great archway flanked by halls, is decorated with fine carvings and intricate screens. In 1948, the last battalion of British troops left India from this gateway.

From there, you will also see an equestrian statue of Chhatrapati Shivaji, the 17th-century Maratha warrior ruler much respected in India for being a bane on the fanatical Mughal emperor Aurangzeb, and a statue of the religious leader Swami Vivekananda.

Walk from the Gateway of India past the Art Deco Dhanraj Mahal to Regal Circle, which has a fine collection of colonial buildings, and cross the road to the museum building.

2 Chhatrapati Shivaji Maharaj Vastu Sanghralaya (formerly Prince of Wales Museum)

See pp108–10.

From the museum gate, follow Mahatma Gandhi (MG) Road to the entrance of Jehangir Art Gallery, one of the most important commercial galleries in Mumbai. On the opposite side of the road is the large National Gallery of Modern Art. Both house exhibitions. Continue to walk along MG Road and turn right on Forbes Street to reach the Knesseth Eliyahod Synagogue.

3 Knesseth Eliyahod Synagogue

This synagogue, built by the Sassoon family in the 1880s, has ornate balconies, and the interiors are beautifully decorated with well-preserved decorations and attractive stained-glass windows.
Tel: (022) 22831502. Open: Mon–Fri 11am–5pm, Sat & Sun 11am–3pm. Return to MG Road and continue to Hutamata Chowk ('Martyr's Square').

4 Flora Fountain

Flora Fountain is one of Mumbai's principal landmarks, with the statue of the Roman Goddess Flora erected in 1899 as a memorial to Sir Bartle Frere who was the governor during Mumbai's urban planning in the 1860s.
Turn right onto Veer Nariman Road.

5 The Cathedral of St Thomas

Considered to be the oldest British building in Mumbai, the Cathedral of St Thomas is a simple but charming church in classical and Gothic styles. Construction began on the church in 1672, but it remained unfinished after the death of Governor Aungier until 1718 when it was finally opened to visitors. Restored at the start of the 2000s, the church has whitewashed interiors with polished wooden furniture and brass, and ornately carved gravestones of British parishioners.
Open: 6.30am–6pm. Free admission.

6 Horniman Circle

To the right of St Thomas church is Horniman Circle, formerly Elphinstone Circle, conceived in 1860 as a centrepiece of the new developments of Mumbai. Around the circle are historic buildings like the neoclassical Town Hall and the Doric Mint of the 1820s, and the Venetian Gothic Elphinstone buildings of the 1870s.
From the west end of Horniman Circle, take Perin Nariman Street which will bring you to CST.

7 Chhatrapati Shivaji Terminus

See p110.

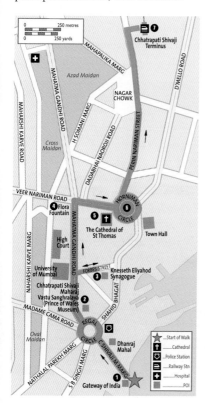

authority on Indian crafts. Started as a museum of economic products, the museum developed into the Victoria & Albert Museum in the 1860s and 1870s. It has been renamed after Ramkrishna Vitthal Lad, known as Bhau Daji Lad, who was one of the people who initiated its development in the 1860s. The museum houses East India Company paintings made for the British, costumes, bronzes, ivory arts and a large collection of maps, prints and models covering the history of Mumbai, including its temples and colonial buildings.

Near Byculla Station. Tel: (022) 23757943. Open: Thur–Tue 10.30am–5pm (last admission 4.30pm). Closed: Wed. Admission charge.

Colaba

Colaba Causeway is one of the city's most crowded thoroughfares leading to the cantonment, which has interesting colonial monuments. One of the most prominent monuments is the Afghan Memorial Church of St John the Baptist, built in the 1840s and 1850s as a memorial to the British who lost their lives in the Afghan Mutiny.

Mahalaxmi

Haji Ali Mausoleum The mausoleum of Haji Ali is a major landmark of Mumbai province with its white dome and minarets. It is set on a tidal island, but a causeway connects it to the mainland during low tide. The

The 'floating' Haji Ali mausoleum

mausoleum houses the tomb of Haji Ali Bukhari, a mystic and saint who is said to have passed away in medieval times near Mumbai on his way to Mecca. The casket containing his remains is believed by devotees to have floated ashore at this place. The structure is currently undergoing renovation, due to be completed towards the end of 2010, so access may be limited.

Opposite Mahalaxmi racecourse.
Accessible at low tide only.
Free admission.

Mahalaxmi Temple The Mahalaxmi Temple, housing idols of goddesses found in the sea who are worshipped here, stands on a headland off Babulnath Desai Road (Warden Road). One of the most visited religious sites, this is a good place to bear witness to Hindu rituals. The Banganga Tank on Malabar Hill is considered one of the city's holiest sites.

Open: approximately 6am–9pm.
Train: Mahalaxmi Station.

Mani Bhavan
Mani Bhavan was the Mumbai base of Mahatma Gandhi from 1917 to 1934. Born in Porbandar in the 19th century, Mahatma Gandhi was schooled at Rajkot and went to college in Bhavnagar before going overseas to pursue his law education. On returning to India in 1915, he launched a non-violent movement for India's freedom struggle, with Ahmedabad as his residence and ashram until 1930.

Then, his march to Dandi protesting against the monopolistic salt act received much public support, breaking the back of the colonial empire in India. This private house where he stayed on visits to Mumbai is now a museum with dioramas depicting scenes from the life of Gandhi, and an exhibition of photos, objects and letters to and from the Mahatma. The interesting collection of letters includes a friendly message to Hitler suggesting world peace, letters to Roosevelt and Tolstoy, and letters from Einstein and Tolstoy. Gandhi's simple belongings are displayed in his room, which also houses his copies of holy books of the Hindus, Muslims and Christians.

19 Laburnum Road, Gamdevi, Mumbai.
Tel: (022) 2380 5864.
www.gandhi-manibhavan.org.
Open: 9.30am–6pm. Admission free.

Marine Drive
The eight-lane Netaji Subash Chandra Road called Marine Drive was built in the 1920s on reclaimed land. The pavement along the sea is a popular promenade of Mumbai, leading from Nariman Point to Chowpatty Beach, alive with street-food vendors and amusements for children, with Art Deco apartment blocks lining the opposite side of the road, and the **Taraporewala Aquarium** (*Marine Drive. Tel: (022) 2282 1239. Open: Tue–Sat 11am–8pm, Sun 10am–8pm. Closed: Mon. Admission charge. Station: Charni Road*) which is one of India's most visited aquariums.

The lights along the promenade, which arcs along the sea towards Malabar Hill, have given it the nickname 'Queen's Necklace'. The beach was the site for many Quit India rallies in the early 20th century when Mumbai was at the forefront of the Freedom Struggle.

M J Phule Market (Crawford Market)
The colonial façade and Gothic towers of this market building, designed by Sir William Emerson whose other great works include the Victoria Memorial, make it a landmark for the market area of Mumbai. The façade has a frieze of workmen in relief carved by John Lockwood Kipling,

Symbolic brass cobra at Walkeshwar Temple

father of author Rudyard Kipling who also lived in this part of Mumbai. The hall is divided into sections dedicated to fruit, vegetables, fish, mutton and poultry. The area around Crawford Market forms a huge bazaar with the cloth markets, Zaveri bazaar, which is the main jewellery market, Abdul Rehman Street, Manish Market and the flower market of Bhuleshwar. This area can be explored for monuments such as the 19th-century Jami Masjid, which is a much-visited mosque, the Mumba Devi Temple that houses the original idol of the goddess who gave Mumbai its name, and the marble Jain temples to Shantinath and Parshwanath near the flower market. The Jains maintain an animal shelter near the temples, Panjarapole, where ill-treated or abandoned pets are kept as well as livestock.
Just north of the CST (Victoria Terminus) Railway Station. Open: Mon–Sat 11.30am–8pm.

Walkeshwar Temple
The temples on the hill leading up from Chowpatty are among the oldest buildings of Mumbai, believed to be about 1,000 years old, but they have been considerably remodelled over the years.

The Walkeshwar Temple is said to have been the resting place of Lord Rama on his way to Lanka to rescue his wife Sita, and the shrine here is said to have been made by him from sand.
Malabar Hill. Free admission.

MUMBAI ENVIRONS
North of Mumbai

Mumbai's northern suburbs are mainly known to tourists for the Kanheri Caves in the Sunjay Gandhi National Park, but there are also some nice beaches and little-known sites of historical significance.

Beaches

One of Mumbai's most popular recreational areas is Juhu beach near the trendy residential neighbourhoods of Juhu, Ville Parle and Bandra. The beach has hotels, restaurants and cafés nearby, and vendors and little eateries close to the seafront.

For a more relaxed getaway from Mumbai, there are beaches at Marve, Manori and Gorai in and around Dharavi Island, about two hours from the centre of Mumbai, which have places to stay and eat. They are also good for birdwatching at the creeks.

Elephanta Caves

The forested island of Elephanta is one of the principal sightseeing attractions for most visitors to Mumbai. The island is reached by boat from Apollo Bunder. The setting is in some ways symbolic, for the sea is an ocean of life with the island providing a spiritual refuge. The caves were excavated more than a millennium ago, though little is known about their origins, and they contain massive carvings depicting the Hindu view of life and spiritualism. It is generally believed that the Shiva cave

temple on Elephanta Island was probably excavated during the 8th century when the Rahtrakuta Dynasty ruled the region, although some of the caves may have had Buddhist origins.

The island was earlier called Garhapuri or Gharapuri but was renamed Elephanta by the Portuguese because they saw a massive elephant sculpture on the island when they captured Mumbai from the Gujarat Sultanate in the 16th century. The caves are known for their graceful monolith sculptures, but many have been damaged by weather, time, invaders and the Portuguese, who allegedly used the caves for target practice. The architectural style shows Gupta and Chalukyan influences.

Elephanta is slightly over an hour by boat from the Gateway of India. Check the time of the last return boat at the ticket desk.

9km (5½ miles) northeast of the Gateway of India. Tel: (022) 2202 6364, (022) 2207 4333 and (022) 2202 4482. Open: Tue–Sun 9am–5pm. Admission charge.

Kanheri Caves

Excavated between the 2nd and the 9th centuries, the Kanheri Caves were mainly residential and meditation areas for monks, but donors ensured that they have some superb carvings. The caves are well designed, with elaborate drainage systems and a water storage system that enabled rain water to be stored in underground tanks. The caves are set on hills in the forests of **Sunjay Gandhi National Park** in Borivali.

There are 109 caves in all, joined to one another by flights of steps, and a few of them are really noteworthy. The first cave is an incomplete *chaitya* hall, signifying that it was to house a *stupa* (Buddhist architectural symbol of enlightenment), while the second has panels showing Buddhas as teachers and the Boddhisattva of compassion, and there are rock-cut beds in the monastic quarters called *viharas*. The third cave is generally considered the most spectacular and significant as it has a *chaitya* hall with a pillared entrance carved with figures of its donors, and a hallway with colonnades around a *dagoba* or domed structure. Some of the pillars have carvings of elephants and trees, and the cave has impressive Buddhas. A cave called the Darbar of the Maharaja has a rest house with stone benches and cells. Cave 11 was probably an assembly hall, with long tables made from rocks used for the study of manuscripts, and Buddha here is depicted as a teacher. Cave 34 has a painting of Buddha in his earth-touching position. Cave 35 was most likely a monastery, and has a relief carving of Buddha. Cave 67 has more Buddha images and also those of the *nagas*, the snake-like forms representing yogis' power. Above the cave complex, a trail leads to the Ashok Van, venerated as a sacred grove of old trees.

The national park has a significant population of leopard and other wildlife, such as spotted deer, barking deer, sambar, wild boar, jackal, hyena and hare, but permission to visit the interior is not easily given. There are some good birdwatching and butterfly spotting trails around the caves. The tourist zone of the park has lion and tiger safari parks.

Admission through Sunjay Gandhi National Park. Open: 7.30am–6pm (park); 9.30am–5.30pm (caves). Admission charge.
Kanheri is about 15km (9½ miles) southeast from Borivali Railway Station on Mumbai's western line.

Ulhasnagar

Ambarnath near Ulhasnagar has a Shiva temple said to date from the 11th century. Though ruined, the temple has impressive sculptures of Shiva as Natraja and as Bhairava, and other deities and celestial dancing women.
Ulhasnagar is accessible by local train from the CST (Victoria Terminus) in Fort. The temple is a five-minute auto-rickshaw ride from Ambarnath Station.

Vasai

Called Bassein by the British, Vasai was the site of the Portuguese conquest of Mumbai when the Portuguese took over the forts built by Sultan Bahadur Shah. It became a port and shipbuilding centre of some significance. Vasai was conquered by the Marathas after a long and devastating battle that took a large toll of lives in 1739. The town has

The tree-covered hills of Sunjay Gandhi National Park

the remains of the old fort with the ruins of a 16th-century cathedral, churches and convents representing various orders.

50km (31 miles) north of Mumbai. Vasai is accessible by local train from Mumbai Central.

Further afield

Pune, southeast of Mumbai, is a historically significant city that has grown to become one of India's most important college cities, industrial cities and software exporters; it is also an army cantonment city. Moreover, the city is significant as a spiritual centre because of its Osho ashram. On the way to Pune from Mumbai, the hill station of Lonavala offers access to interesting Buddhist caves.

Lonavala

The twin hill stations of Lonavala and Khandala attract visitors from Mumbai because of their pleasant climate and landscapes. Lonavala also has one of India's best yoga institutes (*www.kdham.com*). The main draws for tourists are the **Karla and Bhaja caves**. Dating from around the 2nd to

1st centuries BC, these caves are among the finest examples of Buddhist rock-cut carvings in India.

The Karla cave is probably the largest and best-preserved *chaitya* hall (cave with a *stupa*) in India. The stone column at the entrance has four lions, and Buddhist images embellish the interiors. The main hall has kneeling elephants carrying an embracing couple, each carved on the columns. Bhaja has 18 caves with the most significant being cave 12.

Karla Caves: *Karli, near Lonavala. Open: 9am–5pm. Admission charge. Trains from Mumbai take about 3 hours to Lonavala.*

Bhaja Caves: *3km (2 miles) from expressway. Open: 8am–6pm. Admission charge.*

Pune

Pune was the Maratha headquarters from the 1750s, and the British made it their alternative capital to Mumbai in the early 19th century for the summer and monsoon months because of its pleasant weather.

Like Mumbai's Fort area, Pune has imposing British-era buildings such as the 1866 **Raj Bhavan** or **Government House**, the **University building**, the 1840s **All Saints Church**, the **Chapel of St Ignatius**, **Deccan College**, the 1820s **St Mary's Church**, the **Sassoon Hospital**, and the 1860s **Synagogue**.

The historic centre of Pune lies within the old fort walls, with impressive buildings like the **Visram Bagh**, a palatial Maratha building with exquisite woodcarvings, and the **Shaniwar Wada Palace** built in 1736 by the Peshwas.

The **Raja Dinkar Kelkar Museum** (*National Highway 4, opposite DSK Toyota. Tel: (020) 2448 2101. www.rajakelkarmuseum.com. Open: 9.30am–5.30pm. Admission charge*) is one of the highlights of Pune, with an impressive collection of musical instruments, woodcarvings, hookahs, nutcrackers, lamps and temple doors. Pune's tribal museum in the Tribal Research and Training Institute has good documentation of the tribal cultures of Maharashtra and neighbouring states, including a collection of masks, paintings, musical instruments, weapons, woodcarvings, utensils and agricultural implements, besides replicas of tribal houses. The Aga Khan Palace is now the **Kasturba Gandhi Museum** (*Nagar Road, beyond Fitzgerald Bridge. Tel: (020) 2668 0250. Open: 9am–5.45pm. Admission charge*), exhibiting items related to the life of Mahatma Gandhi and his wife, Kasturba, and information about the freedom struggle.

Pune is also a spiritual centre because of the presence of the **Osho Commune** (*17 Koregaon Park. Tel: (020) 6601 9999. www.osho.com. Admission charge*), with the late Bhagwan Rajneesh's ashram continuing to attract visitors for meditation and philosophical discourses. *163km (101 miles) southeast of Mumbai, 475 km (295 miles) north of Panaji.*

Pune is a 50-minute flight from Goa and 40 minutes from Mumbai. By train it is 3–3½ hours to Mumbai and 13–14 hours to Goa.

Sinhagad Fort

This fort, called Sinhagad or Sinhgarh, is often considered an epitome of Maratha warrior skills because it was taken by scaling the cliff at night. The two entrances, Pune Gate and Kalyan Gate, are both protected by successive gates, and two cliffs around the fort have also been fortified.

Open: dawn–dusk.
Sinhagad is about 24km (15 miles) southwest of Pune.

The Aga Khan Palace, now home to the Kasturba Gandhi Museum

MAHARASHTRA'S KONKAN COAST

The Konkan route followed by the Konkan Railway and National Highway 17 from Mumbai to Goa runs between the Western Ghats and the Arabian Sea, and has a string of towns that prospered from the trade through the estuaries of rivers running from the hills to the sea. These towns, with their forts, palaces or other landmarks, make ideal stops on the 593km (369mile) journey from Mumbai to Panaji taken by most travellers to Goa.

Murud Janjira

Murud Janjira is one of the strongest coastal forts of the Konkan, and remained unconquered even by the mighty Maratha warrior rulers like Shivaji and his son Sambaji. The fort is said to have been built in the 12th century by Siddis who came to India from Africa, and Murud Janjira's Siddi rulers were given the hereditary title of Nawab or 'Muslim king' by the Mughal emperors in the 17th century.

The Murud Janjira princely state prospered during British rule, and the Nawabs were granted a 13-gun salute by the empire. The fort is largely ruined and overgrown, but its high walls are impressive, and it contains a mosque, relics of a palace, a cannon house, and watchtowers offering scenic sea views. *www.murudjanjira.com. Open 7am–5.30pm. Charge for the boat ride to the fort.*

Murud Janjira is about 2 hours' drive from Roha on the Konkan Railway route from Mumbai to Margao. Accommodation options along Murud beach.

Ratnagiri

The heart of an important mango-producing zone and a port town, Ratnagiri is famous as the birthplace of Tilak and Gokhale, two of India's best-known freedom fighters during the struggle for independence from British rule. The King of Burma was held here from 1886 to his death in 1916.

You can also visit **Ganpatipule**, a beautiful white-sand beach and an important Hindu religious centre 45km (28 miles) away, the **Jaigad Fort** 55km (34 miles) from the town, and the **Bhagwati Temple** 10km (6¼ miles) from the station.

Ratnagiri is on the main Konkan Railway line from Mumbai to Goa.

Sawantwadi

Sawantwadi was an important nine-gun salute princely state of Maharashtra just near the Goa border. The Bhonsle rulers of Sawantwadi were constantly trying to make inroads into Goa, forcing the Portuguese to build forts to protect their northern territories. Under the Bhonsle rulers, craftspeople thrived, such as the *jindgars* who made richly embroidered saddles, fans and furnishings, the artisans who made lacquered wood products, and the makers of hand-painted playing cards called *ganjifa*. The erstwhile ruling family has converted the **Darbar ('hall of audiences')** at their palace into a workshop for artisans to produce handicrafts, especially the *ganjifa* cards, candlesticks, chess sets, board games and lacquered wooden furniture. The *ganjifa* cards, with their miniature paintings featuring religious and folk themes, make unusual gifts.

Passengers can also alight at Sawantwadi's out-of-town station for **Amboli**, a little hill station with waterfalls and views towards the sea 37km (23 miles) away, and **Redi**, with a village, beach and **Maratha Fort** 20km (12½ miles) from the station and just 3km (2 miles) before the northern border of Goa.

Sawantwadi is on the Konkan Railway line from Mumbai.

The coastal village of Ratnagiri

KOLHAPUR

Though often overlooked by visitors, who bypass it in favour of Goa, the former princely state of Kolhapur has a wealth of attractions to recommend it. Its historical importance has left a splendid architectural legacy, concentrated in the characterful old town. Local people are not yet as blasé about tourism as their counterparts in better known reaches of India, and you are likely to be warmly welcomed. It is also worth a visit for an insight into the architecture and flamboyant lifestyle of 'Princely India' under the 'British Raj'.

The town enjoys an interesting etymology, said to have taken its name from Kolhasur, a demon whose dying wish was to have the place named in his honour. Founded as an independent kingdom in the 18th century, the state flourished after signing treaties with the British Empire. Kolhapur subsequently became something of a model state in the Deccan, with the rulers introducing economic and social reforms, patronising arts and cottage industries, and commissioning schools, colleges and hospitals. It is also of renown as the origin of the piquant Kolhapuri cuisine.

Most of the great city's architectural works date from the 19th century when the British engineer, Charles Mant, was commissioned by the Maharajas (Hindu rulers) to build the palaces, public library, town hall (which now houses an archaeological museum), Albert Edward Hospital and other buildings. The Maharajas were entitled to 19-gun salutes on all formal occasions (only 5 princely states were given the full 21-gun salute and 6, including Kolhapur, were entitled to 19) and led a flamboyant lifestyle maintaining racehorses, elephants for ceremonial processions, Rolls Royces and other cars, and cheetahs trained to hunt fleet-footed antelope.

Kolhapur is about 250km (155 miles) northeast of Panaji by National Highway 4. The city has a good choice of hotels, including the Shalini Palace Hotel, a renovated palace.

New Palace

This impressive palace of the 1880s was designed by Charles Mant in his signature eclectic style featuring Hindu, Islamic and European architecture. The palace is set in parklands with a lake that attracts birds. The stone building is dominated by the huge domes, turrets and Victorian-style watchtower. The palace now houses the **Chhatrapati Shahu Museum**, exhibiting a collection of princely memorabilia, including silver peacock-shaped elephant howdahs (saddles), swings, antique furniture, paintings, a huge armoury of swords, gold-plated weapons, robes, crests, jewellery and stuffed animals. Photographs depict the training of the cheetah, and the hunt, during which a cheetah would be unleashed to course blackbuck antelope. One of the displays shows an elephant readied for a ceremonial procession with decorated

The New Palace, Kolhapur

tusks and elaborate saddles. The centrepiece of the palace is the Darbarhall with its huge chandeliers and carved galleries.
Tel: (0231) 2538060. Open: 9.30am–5.30pm. Admission charge. 3km (2 miles) to the north of the bus and train stations.

Old Town

The old town area of Kolhapur has the old palace, or **Rajwada** (*behind Mahalaxmi Temple. Entrance Hall. Free admission*), of the Maharajas of Kolhapur, dominated by the **Bhavani Mandap** (*open: 6am–8pm. Free admission*). Devotees throng to the **Mahalaxmi Temple** (*open: 5am–10.30pm. Free admission*), said to have been the centre of the tantric cult from the 10th-century Yadav period, which has fine carved towers, domes and an elaborate hall with pillars. Near the temple are the markets for the famous silver and oxidised jewellery, Kolhapuri chappals (slippers and sandals), textiles and jaggery (brown sugar made from the sap of the date palm) of Kolhapur. The city is also known for its wrestlers who can be seen grappling at the gym called Motibagh Thalim near the Bhavani Mandap. Professional wrestling matches take place at Rajarshi Shahu Khasbag Maidan, an arena nearby.

MAHABLESHWAR

The terraced hills of Mahableshwar provide an ideal hill-station getaway for long-staying visitors to Goa. The hill resort was discovered for the British by General Lodwick in the 1820s, and became a regular retreat for British officers and troops stationed in Mumbai and the plains. It even became the summer capital of the British Bombay Presidency.

This hill-resort town has waterfalls, the Venna Lake with boating facilities and a golf course. There are pleasant walks in town and nearby viewpoints like Elphinstone, Babington, Kaste's and Lodwick's points, Wilson Point, which is the popular Sunrise Point, Bombay Point or Sunset Point, and Arthur's Seat, overlooking a precipice towards the Konkan coastal belt.

About 18km (11 miles) from Mahableshwar is Panchgani, which was also a hill station with British and Parsi bungalows. Although better known for its schools, Panchgani is a hill-resort destination for those who want to avoid the holiday rush of Mahableshwar.
Mahableshwar is 300km (186 miles) north of Goa. There are buses to Mahableshwar from Goa. The journey takes 12 hours.

Colonial buildings

As a British summer capital, Mahableshwar has many colonial buildings, including the 1842–67 Christchurch, the Frere Hall, the club, the 1820s Government House and the Beckwith monument. There is also a memorial to the founder, Lodwick.

Pratapgarh

Pratapgarh has a spectacular setting. From the parking area on the road, the climb of 500 steps offers superb views of the forested hillside. The **fort** is protected by dual walls with bastions, the entrance is through gates studded with spikes, and, once inside, the **Bhavani temple** has a pair of lamp towers; the lanterns on the towers may also have worked like beacons. There is a **Shiva temple** inside the fort.

The site of the fort is associated with one of the great tales of Shivaji who is said to have come here to meet a general from Bijapur in the 1650s. It was meant to be a peaceful meeting, but the general came armed and Shivaji killed him with a set of tiger claws that he had wittingly worn on his fingers.
Pratapgarh Fort. Open: 7am–7pm. Admission charge.
About 24km (15 miles) west of Mahableshwar.

Raigadh

Raigadh was the headquarters of the Maratha warrior ruler, Shivaji. Dating from about the 12th century, the fort was ruled by Marathas but fell first to the Vijayanagara rulers and then to the Muslim Sultans. Shivaji conquered it and made it the home of his mother, Jiji Bai. The fort was one of the most powerful in Maharashtra, with heavy fortifications protecting its roughly triangular interiors. The main entrance flanked by bastions leads to the palace with its quarters for the queens and princesses. The fort contains the remains of a market that would have provided the requirements for thousands who stayed in the citadel. A memorial to Shivaji, who died here in the 17th century, is housed in the fort, which also has a Shiva temple with a Nandi bull. The fort has stunning views from its hilltop location.

Open: 8am–5.30pm.
Admission charge.
About 80km (50 miles) northwest of Mahableshwar.

Temples
Mahableshwar has temples to Krishna, Ram and Hanuman. Krishnabai, or Panchganga, is a natural lingam near the Krishna River, and nearby is a 13th-century tank built by a Yadav king.

Impressive scenery around Mahableshwar

Goa's beach resorts

While the entire Goan coastline boasts the same holiday-brochure good looks, with fine white sand, azure waters and lolling palms, individual beaches are strikingly different in atmosphere. This makes it imperative to choose your resort wisely. Hippies, hedonists, party animals, peace-and-quiet-seekers and adrenalin junkies will all find a stretch of sand to suit their requirements.

Northern reaches

If it's a dreadlock holiday you're after, head north. Vying for the accolade of

The beach at Anjuna

Goa's top hippy resort are Arambol and Anjuna. Right at the uppermost tip of the state, Arambol's remoteness keeps its beaches relatively crowd-free, and the place enjoys a warm community spirit. Tie-dyed garments, henna tattoos and nose piercings are out in equal force further down the coast in the more sprawling Anjuna. Chiefly famous for its Wednesday flea market, its honorary title 'Freak Capital of the World' should be enough for the visitor to deduce whether it's likely to be their bag. Anjuna's wide, flat beach, with its atypical dark rock formation, is prime hunting ground for hawkers, while the odd juggler or fire-eater also saunters by. In between Anjuna and Arambol lies low-key Vagator. Despite a lively nightlife, during the day the place is notable for its ruggedness, with dramatic red cliffs offering a splendid sunset view.

Centre-north

Their proximity to the airport led to Goa's central resorts forming the vanguard of mainstream tourism in the state. Calangute and Baga are the two big-hitters. At these package-tour hubs it's all about beach-based fun.

Picture-perfect Palolem

Sunbathing and extreme sports during the day and hard partying when the sun goes down are the order of the day – these are not the right destinations for anyone hoping for a serene holiday. Moving south, Candolim and Sinquerim are noticeably more refined. Candolim has a smattering of watersports on offer, but is far less riotous than its northern neighbours and its beach less busy. It caters to an older crowd, and has a more upmarket feel to its dining and shopping. Sinquerim, to the south, is even posher, with some high-end resorts and top-notch eateries giving the place an exclusive air.

South

South of the capital and airport, the coastal scene gets truly laid-back.

Scruffy Colva and Benaulim are closer to an authentic Indian beach experience, although both still have plenty to offer the tourist. The former fishing village of Colva retains some piscatorial pursuits, adding to its shabby charm. It's relatively bustling, but nothing compared to the frenetic tourist activity going on up north. Slightly further south, Benaulim is quieter, and attracts long-stay visitors who enjoy its paddy-field rusticity. This is the sort of place where you share the sand with cows. Way down at the bottom, picture perfect Palolem has, like Arambol, benefited from its location far from the madding crowd – bookstalls by the beach sum up the relaxed, easygoing ambience. Development is as yet low-key, and there are few distractions to spoil the superlative views.

Getting away from it all

Although Goa is known for the 'travellers' scene' at beaches, it is possible to get away from the crowds by joining Ayurvedic amd yoga programmes, taking up watersports or visiting lakes and wildlife reserves inland.

Boat trips

A number of operators offer boat trips, cruises and watersports such as water-skiing, windsurfing and parasailing. The government has imposed safety regulations, including the provision of life jackets for passengers, but it is best to see the boat before booking a trip.

Crocodile spotting

The tidal waters of the Mandovi River around Chorao and Divar islands support a population of crocodiles. Companies like John's Boat Tours (*Email: john@johnboattours.com. www.johnboattours.com*) offer crocodile-spotting trips down the Cumbarjua canal. Besides looking for crocodiles on the banks, the trip also offers opportunities to see collared and other kingfishers, storks, herons, egrets, redshanks, curlew and other birds, and to see the fiddler crabs, mudskipper fish and other inhabitants of the mangrove habitat.

Cruises

Mandovi River cruises, offered from the Santa Monica jetty by Goa Tourism Development Corporation (GTDC) (*tel: 2427972. Email: gmtc@goa-tourism. com*) and private operators, run for about an hour around sunset. Drinks and snacks can be bought on board from the boat's bar. The highlight of the cruise is usually the performances on board, such as the *Dekni Temple* dance, the *fugdi* dance, the Portuguese *corredinho* dance and Goan music concerts, with the performers dressed in traditional costumes. Full-moon cruises are often operated from the jetty. Some operators also offer cruises to Ribander and Old Goa, with a tour of the monuments, or to the Grande Island from Mormugao. The Backwater Cruise goes upriver along the Salim Ali Bird Sanctuary on Chorao Island, offering views of the mangrove forests with their birdlife and aquatic fauna, and generally includes a Hindu Goan lunch.

Dolphin spotting

Dolphin boat-trip operators generally guarantee sightings of the humped-back dolphins and porpoises that are commonly seen offshore from Goa. *The GTDC organises trips on Saturday if there is demand (tel: 9689917279) (see contact info under Cruises).*

Lakes
Carambolim Lake

Near Old Goa, Carambolim Lake is located between the Mandovi and Zuari rivers, with paddy fields to the south and woods to the west. It is a shallow lake, with plenty of aquatic vegetation and wild rice. The area attracts a multitude of resident and winter birds: purple gallinule, moorhen, white breasted waterhen, purple heron, pond heron, egrets, pratincole, lapwings, ibis, pied and stork-billed kingfishers, spot-billed duck and many other species can be seen for most of the year. In winter the lake is visited by ducks and other migrating waterfowl. Around the lake, birdwatchers can enjoy wagtails, bee-eaters, flameback, woodpeckers, orioles, warblers, pipits, sunbirds, munias, weavers and other species.

3km (2 miles) southeast of Goa Velha.

Getting away from it all

Tourists leaving for a boat trip

Environmental issues

Over the last four decades or so, Goa's economy has grown with the boom in tourism and increasing industrialisation, and these have placed considerable pressure on its fragile ecosystem. Today, the non-governmental organisations (NGOs), activists and journalists have successfully brought green and social issues to the forefront, and environmental, heritage and cultural concerns dominate Goa's politics.

Deforestation

The forests of Goa have been imperilled from the early 20th century, and the problem continued after liberation from Portuguese rule when

Industries such as manganese extraction ...

the government issued licences for large-scale logging of trees in the Western Ghats of the state. Forests have been cleared to make way for commercial plantations, agriculture, mining, roads, residential areas and industry and reservoirs. As a result of such rapid deforestation, many wildlife species are losing their habitats, and the livelihood of tribal groups dependent on forest produce is threatened.

Water

In spite of good rainfall more than twice the national average, water is becoming increasingly scarce in Goa as a result of the rising population and influx of tourists which have led to deforestation in order to build new accommodation, effluents from polluting industries and mines, and the growth of upmarket resorts with spas and pools. The dams built from the 1970s to the 1990s have become contentious issues in Goa because they have not substantially contributed to solving the water shortage problem.

Industry and mines

Large-scale, open-cast mining is one of the largest revenue earners for the state, and accounts for 60 per cent of India's iron ore exports. The scale of mining, however, has adversely affected the environment of Goa, causing soil erosion, deforestation, pollution and pollution-related health problems.

Goa's green lobby points out that each tonne of iron ore extracted from the earth leaves behind two or three times as much mining rejects, rock and soil waste dumped around the mines. During the rains, this waste is flushed into streams and rivers, causing silting of water sources, pollution of freshwater sources and the Khandepar River, the ruin of paddy fields as the red mud slicks affect soil fertility, the smothering of vegetation by dust, and the destruction of marine life as the soil runs into the sea. There is also the question of the sustainability of the industry because the clogging of rivers is affecting the movement of iron ore on the waterways.

Following a petition filed by the Goa Foundation, in 2005 the Supreme Court passed the order that mines operating without environmental clearance would be shut down.

Besides mining, heavy industries around Vasco da Gama and chemical plants near the Carambolim Lake have caused concerns about health hazards for the local people, and damage to the local ecology.

… and cement manufacturing are adversely affecting Goa's environment

Tourism

Goa has grown to become one of the most popular tourist destinations of India, and international and domestic tourism is a valuable source of income for the state and its people. However, such large-scale tourism has had an impact on the environment. The coast is lined with luxury beach resorts that are highly water-intensive, with swimming pools, fountains, gardens and recreational areas, and some of the resorts have been criticised for dumping rubbish and sewage.

Fishing

Overfishing has become a problem in Goa, principally because of large, modern and well-equipped trawlers that are causing fish stocks to dwindle, affecting the livelihood of the 40,000 or so Goans dependent on fishing for their livelihood. Overfishing increases the prices of fish and other seafood, and causes marine pollution.

Mayem Lake

This lake in Bicholim is attractively located in a pleasant valley, just before the mining areas to the east, and has traditionally been a popular spot for pedal boating, picnics and birdwatching, although it has suffered from neglect of late.

2km (1¼ miles) south of Bicholim.

The natural world

Bhagwan Mahavir Sanctuary and Molem National Park

Molem is one of the most organised areas for wildlife viewing in Goa. Jeeps are usually parked near the interpretation centre where permission can be obtained, for a nominal entry fee, to visit the Bhagwan Mahavir Sanctuary and Molem National Park. Gaur (or Indian bison) is the species most likely to be seen, but there are also chances of seeing spotted deer, wild boar, langur, rhesus macaques and bonnet monkeys, and striped-neck mongoose. Molem is also the starting point for hikes to Dudhsagar Falls, Atoll Gad, Matkonda Hill and Tambdi Surla. A number of Western Ghats' endemic birds and reptiles can be seen while driving or trekking in the forests.

The Dudhsagar Spa Resort (www.dudhsagarsparesort.com) can arrange visits to the sanctuary and other attractions in the area. To arrange a visitor's permit, contact the Range Forest Officer. Tel: 2612211. www.goaforest.com and www.goa-tourism.com.

Open: 8.30am–5.30pm. Admission charge. About 60km (37 miles) southeast of Panaji and 50km (31 miles) east of Margao Station.

Spot a rhesus macaque in Molem National Park

Deer can often be seen at Goa's sanctuaries

Getting away from it all

Bondla Sanctuary

The **Bondla Sanctuary** has a zoological park as its focal point, but the forests are also inhabited by leopard, gaur, jungle cat, leopard cat, civet, sambar, spotted deer, wild boar, porcupine, pangolin (scaly anteater), Malabar giant squirrel, draco flying lizard and a variety of birds. To see the wildlife, plan to come early – before the crowds visit the park – when the state mammal, the gaur, and the state bird, the ruby-throated yellow bulbul, may be seen. The interpretation centre has information on the sanctuary and the forest department operates simple accommodation at their ecotourism centre at Bondla.

Interpretation centre. Tel: 2610022. www.goaforest.com. Open: Fri–Wed 9am–5.30pm. Admission charge. About 52km (32 miles) northeast of Panaji.

Cotigao Sanctuary

This 105sq km (40^1/$_2$sq mile) sanctuary has an impressive checklist of mammals, but they are hard to spot. It is a good site for watching birds, with watchtowers at canopy level – but take care on the ladders.

Tel: 2750246. Open: 7am–5.30pm. www.goaforest.com. Admission charge. About 52km (32 miles) southwest from Margao Station.

Dandeli Wildlife Sanctuary

Many rivers flow through this sanctuary, including the Kali, which has become popular for river rafting. The river starts above the Dudhsagar Falls and flows through forests to its east before turning west towards the sea. Grey-headed fish eagle, lesser adjutant stork, darter, herons, lapwings and other birds may be seen along the rivers, while the forests are home to tigers, leopards and elephants.

Resorts and upmarket camps offer accommodation and sanctuary tours (*www.junglelodges.com and www.indianadventures.com*). Tel: (022) 26408742. Open: 6am–6pm. www.dandeli.com. *About 50km (31 miles) east of Molem.*

Mhadei Wildlife Sanctuary

This 208sq km (80sq mile) sanctuary near Satari in northern Goa joins the Bhagwan Mahavir Sanctuary and the forests of neighbouring Maharashtra.

About 70km (43 miles) northeast of Panaji and 106km (66 miles) northeast of Margao.

Salim Ali Bird Sanctuary

This bird sanctuary can be explored during the backwaters cruise generally offered by Goa Tourism Development Corporation (*see p130*) or during the boat trips run by Southern Birdwing (*see p130*) for crocodile spotting and birdwatching.

Open: 6am–6pm. Admission charge. 4km (2½ miles) east of Panaji. This sanctuary is also accessible by boat from Ribandar; allow at least one and a half hours for boat trips.

Devbagh Island

Devbagh Island is associated with the Nobel Prize-winning poet Rabindranath Tagore, who wrote his first play *Prakritir Pratishoota*, or *Nature's Revenge*, at the beach on the island. The island has cottage accommodation on the beach, and has developed into a popular centre for watersports.

Trains run from Margao to Karwar, from where it is a short boat journey to Devbagh.

Jog Falls

Goa has impressive waterfalls like Dudhsagar, but the highest waterfall

You might be lucky enough to spot wild elephants

White-water rafting is a popular activity in Dandeli Wildlife Sanctuary

in India is Jog Falls in Karnataka. The Jog Falls have four falls, with the longest dropping 253m (830ft), although the dam on the Sharavati River has reduced the flow. The falls are set in the spectacular countryside of the jungle carpeted hills of the Western Ghats, with good hiking.

32km (20 miles) northwest of Sagara. Trains run from Margao to Karwar, from where it is a 6-hour journey by bus to Jog Falls. There is simple accommodation at Jog Falls.

Yoga

As yoga has gained global popularity, well-known yoga teachers now hold classes at destinations such as Goa, targeting tourists who want to join a course or brush up on their yoga. Many of these are temporary schools that set up during the winter months when Goa's tourist arrivals are at their peak. Candolim, Anjuna, Arambol, Vagator, Benaulim and Palolem are some of the beaches where centres offer courses in Prayanama, Ashtanga, Hatha and other forms of yoga and meditation, and there are also centres near towns such as Margao. Unless you have a good recommendation for a yoga centre, check the credentials of the teacher or ask for a trial before enrolling. Some upmarket resorts at Arossim, Benaulim, and other beaches of South Goa also offer yoga lessons.

Ayurveda and spas

Ayurveda, a holistic form of medicine with origins in the Indian hills, is hugely popular in Goa. Besides treatments and rejuvenation therapies, Ayurvedic centres offer relaxing massages. The government has laid down stipulations for cleanliness and staff qualifications, and ensures that ethical practices and approved Ayurvedic centres have been certified, but it is advisable to check the standards before joining a programme.

Many hotels and resorts have set up Ayurvedic centres, and offer other spa treatments.

The word *Ayurveda* is derived from the Sanskrit words for 'wisdom', or 'science', or 'life', and the philosophy is based on a holistic understanding of

Dhara – an Ayurvedic treatment involving a flow of herbal oil onto the patient's forehead

the human body, mind and spirit; illness affects both the body and the mind, and these should therefore not be treated separately. Physical and emotional health can be maintained by balancing energies, and diagnosis is based on the philosophy that illness is the result of a loss of balance of doshas, a combination of elements that comprise the human body, making use of the 107 *marmas* or sensitive points. Ayurvedic physicians prescribe traditional healing techniques such as purification, diet, herbal medicine, massage, meditation and yoga.

Ayurveda was discouraged by the British Raj, but following independence in 1947 the government of India promoted it as an important form of medicine.

For most visitors to Goa, the most enjoyable and relaxing Ayurvedic treatment is a massage, which is also the first cleansing therapy offered to most patients as a form of pre-detoxification. Primarily a form of medicine, the relaxing effect of massage is secondary. The massage oils have properties that help to heal and protect the skin; the therapist uses gentle, circular movements – with the degree of pressure depending on the patient's condition – covering the head and the body, and the massage is followed by a steam bath. Some resorts also offer synchronised massages by two or more therapists, as well as Chavatti-Uzhichil, which is done by foot instead of by hand, for rejuvenation, muscle toning, weight loss and improved circulation.

The Ayurvedic programmes offered by most hotels and resorts are *Rasayana Chikitsa* (rejuvenation therapy), *Kayakalpa Chikitsa* (body immunisation and longevity therapy), *Sveda Karma* (involving body cleansing by inducing perspiration as part of pre-detoxification) and *Panchakarma* (for overall well-being). Many resorts provide programmes for patients suffering from rheumatic and arthritic problems, backache and chronic ailments. Meditation, yoga and stress-relief programmes are also popular.

Another treatment on offer at Ayurvedic resorts is *Dhara*. In *Sirodhara*, a thin flow of herbal oil, from a pot with a hole suspended over the patient's head, is directed to a spot on the forehead near the eyebrows and then stroked down the hair by the therapist and allowed to permeate the skin. The oil may be massaged into the scalp if prescribed by the physician. Other forms of *Dhara* involve the pouring of buttermilk, fermented yoghurt-based fluids or medicated milk over the forehead or body.

Shopping

Shopping is a quintessential part of the Goan experience. The state boasts a wealth of tempting souvenirs, in the form of clothes, bags, textiles and handiwork. It is something of a national hub, with wares flooding in from Kashmir, Tibet, Nepal, Gujarat, Rajasthan and Southern India. The retail epicentre is the famous Anjuna hippie market, an enormous bazaar that attracts colourful traders of all kinds. Even if you don't buy anything it's a great spectacle and experience. Other resorts have smaller amounts of the same stuff.

How to shop

At established shops, prices are generally fixed and there is no real room for bargaining, although some shops will give you a deal for large purchases. Shops usually announce 'clearance sales', 'discount sales', 'off-season sales' and 'festival discounts' in the newspapers or declare them on banners.

At street-side markets and at flea markets the prices are usually marked up and there is considerable room for bargaining. In tourist centres, vendors generally hike the price up and you might do well by halving the asking price and then reaching an agreement. Walk away slowly in order to gauge the response of the vendor, and you will usually be called back for further negotiation. Shop owners and sales people can be very persuasive, so it is important to be firm and not be swayed.

What to buy

Hippie-inspired clothes, bags and throws pour forth from almost every shop and stall that a tourist might happen upon. Well known for its plantations, Goa has excellent cashew nuts and locally grown spices, which can be bought at shops in towns such as Panaji, Ponda, Margao and Mapusa. Though the state is not renowned for its handicrafts, you could buy painted tiles called *azulejos* from workshops or art galleries. You can also find good tailors in Goa who are used to stitching garments to order.

It is illegal to take genuine antiques out of India without proper licensing, but you can find good copies in the markets.

Where to buy

Government-owned emporia are generally safe bets for genuine quality at fixed prices, but sometimes private shops also claim to be government emporia. Hotel shopping malls and big shops also guarantee quality, although they may be more expensive.

Travellers who feel they may miss out on good bargains by shopping from established shops can check the prices at the government emporia and use them as benchmarks.

Old city bazaars are atmospheric and full of colour, and the maze of streets and alleys is lined with vendors, open-air stalls and shops selling a wide range of products for the locals, including utensils, jewellery, clothes and food.

Goa also has flea markets like the one at Anjuna where you may find something interesting or useful, and other local markets are certainly good value. Night markets like the one at Arpora are popular with travellers.

You can also do well by looking in shops meant for locals, which are usually competitively priced, especially those away from the main tourist centres.

With the increasing flow of tourists and Goans working overseas, Goa has also become a market for branded goods which can be bought on 18th June Road in Panaji, Calangute, along the coastal stretch between Candolim and Baga, and in Southern Goa. 'Lifestyle stores', selling art, reproduction antiques, handicrafts, furniture and crockery, have opened in locations like Sangolda, and are usually housed in stately Goan houses.

Art and antiques
The Attic
Fermen H No 69, Acoi Road, near Mount Carmel Chapel, Camarcazana, Mapusa. Tel: 2257743. Email: css-goa@sacharnet.in
Casa Goa
Khobra Vaddo, Baga Road, Calangute.
Tel: 2281048.
Email: casagoa_india@hotmail.com

Contemporary art galleries
Art Chamber
Art gallery featuring different artists.
115a Gauravaddo, Calangute.
Tel: 2277144.
Kerkar Art Gallery
Gallery which holds performances, exhibitions and workshops.
Holiday Street, Gauravaddo, Calangute.
Tel: 2276017. Email: kerkarart@
gmail.com. www.subodhkerkar.com
Panjim Inn & Panjim Pousada
E-212, 31 Janeiro Road, Fontainhas,
Panjim. Tel: 2226523.
www.panjiminn.com

Books
Broadway Book Centre
Ashirwad Building, next to Rizvi Tower,
18th June Road, Panaji. Tel: 6647038,
www.broadwaybooksgoa.com
Confidant Bookstore
Rua Abade Faria, behind the Lawrence & Mayo shop, Margao. Tel: 2732450.
Other India Bookstore
Highly reputed, stocking titles from Asia, Africa and Latin America.
Above Mapusa Clinic, Mapusa.
Tel: 2263306. Email: admin@
otherindiabookstore.com.
www.otherindiabookstore.com
The Oxford Bookstore
152 Apeejay House, Shop 39/12
Haddows Road, Calangute.
Tel: 9326060647. Email: oxfordgoa@
apeejaygroup.com

Reading Habit

Ag 1 & 2, New Horizon, Plot No B-3/4, St Mary's Colony, DB Marg, Miramar. Tel: 2463057.

Singbal Bookstall

Communicade Building, Church Square, near Our Lady of the Immaculate Conception, Panaji. Tel: 2425747.

Varsha

Azad Maidan, Omuz Road, Panaji. Tel: 2425832.

Department stores

Saga

Opp. Dona Sylvia resort, Khandi Mobor Road, Cavelossim. Tel: 2871417. www.sagastores.com

Handicrafts

Aparant

State-run handicraft network with outlets in Panjim, Vasco da Gama, Margao, Mapusa, Calangute, Bicholim and Lontolim.

Tel: 2226448.

Carlo Menze Collections

For ceramics, cabinets and Chinese arts.

54 Rua Sao Tome. Tel: 2231241. www.carlomenze.com

Heirlooms

Selling ceramic and other handicrafts.

XIII Junta House, 18th June Road, Panaji. Tel: 2224788.

Manthan

Lifestyle store, with antiques, paintings and handicrafts.

1346 Manzil Vaddo, near Holy Trinity Church, Benaulim. Tel: 2771659.

Nyara

Textiles and handicrafts shop.

H561, Orgao, Near Miranda House, Loutolim. Tel: 2777175.

Villa Saligao

This cottage-industry emporium sells a wide variety of handicrafts.

H295 Piqueno Morod, Chogem Road, Saligao. Tel: 2409756.

Garments and boutiques

Archana

Indian designer dresses.

15 Padmavati Towers, 18th June Road, Panaji. Tel: 2420898.

Bandhej

Contemporary and traditional clothes.

Navalkar Trade Centre 5–19, opp. Azad Maidan, MG Road, Panaji. Tel: 2421323.

Caro Centre

Clothes shop.

Abade Faria Road, near Municipal Gardens, Margao. Tel: 2705659.

Cocoon Art Gallery

Designer clothes and art.

E/6 27 Cobra Waddo, near Milky Way, Calangute.

Fab India

Delightful shop selling all sorts of western and Indian clothes plus souvenirs. Despite its understandable popularity with tourists it is still great value. There is also a Panaji branch, off DB Marg, Campal.

Seashell Arcade, opposite Canara Bank, Murrod Vaddo, Candolim. Tel: 2489143. www.fabindia.com

Raymonds
Men's clothes shop.
Isidoro Baptista Road, near Blue Pearl
Theatre, Margao. Tel: 2711501.
www.raymondindia.com

Sosa's
E-245 Rua de Oorum, Panaji.
Tel: 2228063.

Svelte
Boutique, with another outlet in Panaji.
5 Midland Apartments, Miguel Loyola
Furtado Road, Margao. Tel: 2715674.
www.svelteapparel.com

Velho e Filhos
Branded garments.
Opp. Municipal Garden, Panaji.
Tel: 2425338.

Gifts and stationery

Paperworks
F/1 Pinto Arcade, opp. Gymkhana
Campal, DB Marg, Panaji.
Tel: 2425841.

Jewellery

Chirag Jewellers
19 Shar N Sorai Building, VV Road,
Margao. Tel: 2734104.

Hardalikar Jewellers
Mapusa. Tel: 2262484.

Intergold
9 Mascarenhas Building, MG Marg,
Panaji. Tel: 5642882.

Lifestyle

Camelot
Designer dresses and handicrafts.
139 Fondvem, Ribandar Road.
Tel: 2444503.

Sangolda
Attractive lifestyle shop.
E-26 Chogm Road, Sangolda.
Tel: 2409309.

Music

Pedro Fernandes
19 Av D João Castro, GPO, Panaji.
Tel: 2226642.

Rock n Raaga
25 Rizvi Towers, 18th June Road, near
Pharmacy College, Panaji. Tel: 2422841.

Sinari's
18th June Road, Panaji. Tel: 2224842.

Vibes
Anna Felicia, Custodio Pinho Road,
Comba, Margao. Tel: 2705116.

Textiles

Co-optex
EDC house, Dr. Atmaram Borker,
Panaji. Tel: 2220128. www.cooptex.com

Buddha for sale

Arts and crafts

Although Goa does not have a distinctive legacy of a school of painting, and is not particularly well known for its handicrafts, the continuous flow of travellers to the state has made it a large market for contemporary arts, including those of Goan artists, and handicrafts from around the country.

Art and design

Goa has associations with many contemporary artists, including Dr Subodh Kerkar who owns an art gallery, Odette Gonsalves whose forte is painting powerful horses, Harshada Kerkar, Viraj Naik, Santosh Morajkar, Chaitali Morajkar, Pradip Naik, Theodore Mariano Mesquita, Shireen Mody, Liesl Cotta De Souza and Querozito De Souza who exhibit regularly. The famous cartoonist, artist and illustrator Mario Miranda is one of Goa's best-known citizens. His illustrations can be seen everywhere from hotel lobbies through book covers to albums, and souvenirs with reproductions of his works can be bought in Goa. Goa is also the home of Alexyz, the cartoonist whose contributions can be seen in Goan and other newspapers, and Carl D'Silva who has illustrated many leading field guides to the birds of India. The art galleries at Panjim Inn and Panjim Pousada, Velha Goa Galleria and Gallery Rallino, all in Panjim, exhibit and sell contemporary paintings. Panjim also has an art college of note.

Many well-known designers live and work in Goa, and their fashion garments and accessories are available at stores in different locations of the state (see pp140–43).

Azulejos

Azulejos are the famous Portuguese-influenced hand-painted tiles that can be seen at the library in Panaji. These tiles are still painted in workshops in Goa, and can be bought at the art galleries in Panjim.

Buddhist curios

Tibetan vendors have become a feature of Goa, and they sell metal

Handcrafted goods on display

Buddhist curio reproductions such as masks and Buddha images, *thangkas* (Buddhist paintings) and utensils.

Carpets

As Kashmiris have set up many plush handicraft emporia in Goa, it is easy to find their carpets and rugs, which are among the finest in the world. Carpets are usually made of wool, silk or 'silk touch wool'.

Carvings

Woodcarvings and stone sculpture, usually devotional Hindu art from South India, are easily available in Goa at the emporia, and you can also find artisans working on them at the markets.

Jewellery

Handcrafted jewellery from Rajasthan, Gujarat, Tibet and South India is available at handicraft stores, bazaars and flea markets in Goa. At the flea markets and weekly markets, Lambanis from neighbouring Karnataka come to sell their silver, bead and old coin jewellery.

Musical instruments

A variety of Indian musical instruments is sold at stores in Panaji and other towns, and sometimes in emporia at hotels. Second-hand musical instruments sometimes turn up for sale at the flea markets.

Art galleries exhibit contemporary paintings

Papier-mâché

A characteristic Kashmiri art, papier-mâché is available at most emporia in Goa. The item is moulded in layers before painting and polishing to produce the final design. The work can be very intricate, and articles produced include pots, jewellery boxes, Christmas tree baubles, bowls, cups, containers, lamps, coasters and trays.

Textiles

A number of Gujarati and Marwari traders live and work in Goa selling handicrafts of Gujarat- and Rajasthan-influenced embroideries, block-prints, *bandhani* (tie-and-dyed fabrics) and appliqué bedcovers. A variety of other handloom-woven textiles from Kashmir to Kerala is available in Goa.

Entertainment

Most people who come to Goa will find entertainment enough on its striking beaches, in its shimmering waters and, after dark, in the numerous Bob Marley-venerating beach shacks. But the state isn't just about the sand and sun – there's a lively cultural scene too. Goa's vibrant music and dance will provide a memorable holiday soundtrack. Bollywood has made its mark here too, and you can even gamble away your rupees and dollars – a rare opportunity in conservative India.

Casinos

Goa is one of the few states in India where gaming facilities are legal, and many five-star beach hotels and resorts have their own gaming areas, sometimes offering free casino coupons as part of their off-season packages. Goa also has a growing number of floating casinos. Typically gamblers board in the early evening, paying a fixed fee that covers entry, a buffet meal, some drinks and live entertainment. The boat cruises up and down the Mandovi until the early hours, with small tenders taking passengers back to shore at frequent intervals. Two big names in the game are the MV *Caravela* and MV *Casino Royale*.

Caravela. Fisheries Jetty, Dayanand Bandodkar Marg. Tel: (0832) 2234044. www.caravelabeachresort.com. Open: Mon–Thur 5.30pm–5am, Fri–Sun 5.30pm–6am. Admission charge.

Casino Royale. Tel: 6659400. www.casinoroyalegoa.com. Open: 6pm–8am. Admission charge.

Cinema

India has one of the world's largest film industries, dubbed Bollywood as it is based in Mumbai (Bombay), which produces around 1,000 Hindi films a year. While Hindi films transcend regional borders, doing well in most states of India, regional-language film industries in Andhra Pradesh, Tamil Nadu, Karnataka, West Bengal and other states are also thriving. The films have large audiences, and stars have a large fan following, achieving almost cult status; in the south, some have even been elevated to the levels of gods. Their popularity has made the actors politically influential and some have achieved positions of power. They are often called upon for canvassing during state and national elections.

A Hindi film is usually a larger-than-life escapist fantasy, though in recent times stories have become more realistic. While tragedies were popular in the early years of the Hindi film industry, the 1970s and 1980s saw the advent of 'masala movies', which followed set formulae that appealed across cultural boundaries. Common themes were: a hero, the 'angry young man', fighting evil against all odds with a love interest thrown in; a reunion between brothers separated during childhood; or one of the 'love triangle' themes involving two friends in love with the same girl, with one making the 'supreme sacrifice' for his friend.

Spanning three hours including an interval, a typical Hindi film features a little of everything – romance, comedy, action, melodrama, religious piety and song sequences at the drop of a hat, usually filmed in spectacular settings such as snowy peaks, desert dunes or beaches. Many films are shot in foreign

Film Posters at the International Film Festival of India

Sitar and Tebele players playing Raga, a traditional Indian style of music

locations, and one producer was even given an award by a foreign tourism board for making their destination popular in India.

Today, the film industry is going through something of a revolution with film-makers targeting the Hindi-speaking audience in the UK and USA, as well as in other countries where tickets are more expensive than in India and DVDs are in greater demand. The increased revenues have resulted in better production standards and more subtle story lines.

In India, Hindi films continue to be popular, and there is a cinema hall in or near every village. The standards of cinema halls are improving in the larger cities of India, with many new multiplexes offering more legroom and more comfortable seats. The Inox in Panaji has been joined by other multiplexes – check reviews in newspapers to make an educated choice before heading for the cinema. Some also show Hollywood hits.

The International Film Festival of India (IFFI) was held in Goa for the first time in 2004, with films screened at the Inox, at the Kala Academy and at open-air venues such as parks and beaches. Panaji was decorated for the occasion with street lamps, fountains and an improved walkway along the riverfront, and an illuminated jetty was set up behind the Kala Academy for delegates who chose to arrive by boat from the hotels on the coast. Indian and foreign films were shown and live outdoor music concerts were well received. The IFFI was held there again in 2005, and it was decided that Goa would henceforth be its permanent home. In 2009, the 40th edition of the festival also included events in Margao.

Cultural centres

Kala Academy is Goa's main cultural centre, comprising: The Faculty of Indian Music, teaching classical vocal and instrumental music; the Department of Western Music, started as Academia de Musica in 1952; The School of Dance, where Bharatnatyam, Kathak and other Indian classical dances are taught; and the School of Drama, or Faculty of Theatre Art. The academy regularly organises classical and contemporary dance performances, music concerts, plays and exhibitions. Designed by award-winning architect Charles Correa, the Kala Academy has an indoor auditorium where most classical music and dance performances are staged, and an outdoor amphitheatre for plays, music concerts, school gatherings, orchestras and competitions. The academy can be a good place to see regional theatre, music, dance and other performances. Marathi and Konkani performing arts festivals take place at the academy. The centre regularly hosts films as part of the IFFI (see p148). Programmes are announced in local newspapers.
D Bandodkar Marg, Campal, Panaji. Tel: 2420452.

Just a few minutes walk from Calangute beach, the Kerkar Art Complex has regular Indian classical concerts, dance performances and other cultural programmes.

Gaurawado, Calangute. Tel: 2276017. www.subodhkerkar.com

Nightlife

Many hotels, resorts and restaurants have live bands or employ singers on most nights to entertain diners. Goans love to party and the scene can get lively during festivals, feasts and the Carnival.

Goa also has bars, discos and casinos, mostly at hotels and resorts. Evening cruises with on-board cafeteria and bar, and short performances of local music and dance, continue to be popular, but they can be a little disappointing. Nightclubs are mostly to be found in the luxury resorts of South Goa, where they cater to well-heeled Indian and foreign tourists. Campal in Panaji, Calangute and Anjuna also have nightclubs.

Parties

Goa has been known for 'travellers' parties' at the beaches, but these sometimes got out of hand and were often raided by authorities if they suspected drugs were present. The parties were generally all-night affairs, especially during the full moon, at beaches such as Anjuna and Vagator. The parties were hugely popular in the early 1990s, but since the government imposed restrictions, parties are closed down if they exceed their allotted time. Some clubs have permanent party venues, but you need a personal recommendation to find a good one.

Children

Though not a traditional family holiday destination for Westerners, India in general is becoming increasingly popular with alternative-minded parents keen to open their children's eyes to the wider world and Eastern culture. Goa, with its well established tourist network, ease of getting around and great beaches, is a natural choice. A family-oriented society, Indians welcome children and those with them. That said, travelling in Goa does involve some difficulties and hazards of which parents in particular should be aware.

Accommodation

It makes sense to find a good hotel for your base while in India. Most chefs will prepare food to your requirements and there is usually a mini-bar with bottled water and snacks. Hotels will happily supply an extra bed or a family room at a supplement, although children below the age of ten are not usually charged for occupying a room. Some hotels and resorts are geared up for children, with play areas, toddlers' pools, indoor games, movies, competitions and special menus, but it is best to find out about the facilities when you book. Some hotels may be able to arrange babysitters.

Food

Although formula milk and baby food are available in Goa, it may be a good idea to carry some with you, especially if your child has particular favourites. At hotels, resorts and restaurants there is generally a large menu, with good options for children. Eggs, biscuits, bread, butter, cheese, chocolate, bottled drinks, ice cream, packaged and canned foods are generally available everywhere.

Health

Those travelling with babies and children need to be careful. Besides all the necessary vaccinations (*see p183*), children should also be protected against diphtheria, whooping cough, mumps, measles and hepatitis B.

Local people love children and will offer them sweets and fruits, so it is important to be vigilant about this when travelling with children. It may help to explain if a child has to be on a special diet when travelling in India.

One of the major concerns for visitors with children is the sun, which even in winter or in cloudy weather can cause severe sunburn. Use sunhats and sunblock cream at all times.

Children

On the road

Long journeys with children in India can be difficult, so it is best to base yourself in just one or two places. If you are renting a car, buying a child's car seat is a good idea. Bathrooms are rarely clean; taking a portable toilet seat with you may help. There are grocery stores on the roadside, and snacks are available on board the trains, but it is best to pack some snacks for your journey. Biscuits, chocolates and soft drinks are easily available.

Your children may be disturbed by the attention lavished on them by Indians, so be prepared for this.

Packing

Nappies and toiletries are available in Indian cities, but emergency supplies are recommended. Also, make sure you bring any medicines which you may need, as well as a first-aid kit. It is a good idea to pack some toys and books to keep children amused.

Things to do

India does not have any of the large amusement parks that children look forward to visiting. However, they will probably enjoy the general liveliness of India, where getting around in auto-rickshaws, trains, ferries and chartered boats can be fun. Rides on elephants, camels, ponies and boats are also great favourites.

Backwaters

Cruising the backwaters can be great fun for children, and speedboats can also be hired for short journeys.

Beaches

Goa's coastline is lined with excellent beaches and you are really spoilt for choice. The northern beaches are usually more popular and crowded, with beach restaurants and shacks, while the southern beaches are mainly visited by those staying at the hotels and upmarket beach resorts that overlook them. The beaches near

Don't forget sun protection if you take the kids on a boat trip

Panaji, such as Dona Paula and Miramar, are popular locally. Most beach resorts cater for children and even organise activities such as sandcastle competitions. Before entering the water, check that it is safe to swim or paddle there; some beaches have lifeguards who will show you the safest areas.

Boat trips

A number of boat trips are on offer from Goa, including dolphin or crocodile viewing. Many lakes have paddle-boat facilities.

Schoolboy selling candles outside a church

In town

All cities and towns have parks and gardens, with paths for a pleasant stroll and with areas for children to play.

Shopping

The Indian bazaars and handicraft emporia can be fun for children, though you should take care in crowded markets. Locally made dolls dressed in the costumes of different states of India, papier-mâché masks, handcrafted wooden toys and miniature boats are favourites. However, make sure that the toys you buy are safe for children.

Wildlife reserves

In Goa, Molem is the centre of wildlife-viewing activities. There are a few hotels and camps at Molem, and also at nearby Tambdi Surla, which can arrange visits to the Bhagwan Mahavir Wildlife Sanctuary. Indian bison and deer are generally seen during short drives. Bondla is more popular as a zoo than as a wildlife sanctuary, unless you visit early in the morning when deer herds are active.

Though wildlife reserves like Molem and Cotigao have an impressive list of mammals, seeing any of the big ones is not easy. The neighbouring state of Karnataka has wildlife reserves such as Dandeli, Bhadra, Nagarhole and BR Hills where elephant sightings are possible; leopards, tigers and bears have also been seen by some lucky visitors.

Indian dolls are a favourite with children

Sport and leisure

Sport is a high priority for most Goans. Although sports are not generally associated with India, except, of course, for cricket and Himalayan mountaineering, they are nevertheless a popular form of entertainment. All kinds are on offer, from spectator sports to those especially developed for tourism, such as watersports and adventure activities. New-age pursuits, such as yoga and Ayurvedic massages, also have a huge following in Goa.

Large hotels and resorts have sports facilities including swimming pools, and many smaller ones have indoor games facilities such as pool tables. The clubs are the best places for sports and leisure, but entry is usually restricted to members. Some clubs have reciprocal arrangements with those elsewhere, while some offer temporary membership, and hotels may be able to arrange admission to a club nearby. Some clubs also have residential rooms, which can be an alternative to staying at hotels, but you may need to be introduced by a member. You could also ask about government-run sports facilities that are open to the general public.

SPORTS FACILITIES
Adventure sports and watersports

Watersports operators offer activities seasonally at Northern Goan beaches such as Sinquerim, Candolim and Calangute, and at some beaches in Southern Goa (Colva, Utorda, Benaulim and Mobor), but it is important to inspect the equipment or ask about safety standards.

Parasailing is popular along the Sinquerim-Calangute stretch of coast, which offers views of Fort Aguada while airborne. Jet-skiing, water-skiing and windsurfing are also regular features of Goa in the peak season.

For rafting, Dandeli National Park in Karnataka is easily accessible from Goa. The rafting activities on offer range from scenic floats through the forests, which are good for birdwatching and occasional wildlife sightings, to strenuous white-water rafting at the falls. There are resorts and camps near the entrance to the national park.

Angling
Some hotels and resorts have their own ponds, private lakes or backwater inlets where they allow fishing on a 'catch-and-release' or 'you-catch-we-cook' basis. Most of them have fishing rods,

but it may be a good idea to bring your own equipment. Deep-sea fishing trips may be possible with local fishermen.

Neighbouring Karnataka offers angling trips on the Cauvery in quest of the mahseer, one of the most sought-after game fish.

Basketball

Basketball is a popular game, mainly at school and college level in Goa.

Billiards and snooker

Billiards and snooker are popular in India (among those who can afford to play). Most clubs have a billiards room and some hotels have pool tables.

Cricket

Cricket is the most popular sport in India. Crowds gather in hotels and public places to watch international fixtures on TV, especially if the Indian team is playing. You can observe cricket practice at stadiums and campuses, as well as informal games played on open ground, and children playing with a bat and ball even in narrow streets. You may even be invited by locals to join a friendly game. At

Scratch game of cricket at sunset, Candolim

Jet-skiing at Calangute

competitive level, cricket is a serious business, and Indian clubs invite foreign teams to play or tour other countries.

Cycling

Goa offers a variety of terrain for bicycle touring. Indian bicycles are good for short distances and local sightseeing, but they are not very comfortable for serious touring on hilly roads or rocky paths. You can either join a group tour with everything taken care of by the operator, or bring your own bicycle, preferably a mountain bike. If you bring a bicycle, carry more spares than you think will be needed, as well as oil and a pump.

Indian cycles can be hired at most cities, towns and villages at nominal prices. Imported cycles are available only at very popular tourist destinations in Goa.

Football

Football is a popular sport in Goa. In winter, Goan villages play league games, with sponsored teams such as Salgaocar, Dempo, Sesa Goa and Churchill Brothers. The Nehru Stadium at Fatorda near Margao is one of the largest football centres on India's west coast, seating about 35,000. Details of matches are published in the newspapers. Foreign players, especially those from African countries, also take part in Goa's football season.

With the advent of international TV channels in India, football is widely followed in the country, and most locals will discuss the last World Cup if they know you have any interest in the game. Brazilian football stars have a large fan following in Goa.

Golf

Many resorts in Goa have their own nine-hole golf courses or can arrange for guests to play at one of the clubs nearby. Mumbai has a number of golf courses, but most of them are only accessible to members.

Scuba diving

Goa has diving schools, certified by the Professional Association of Diving Instructors (PADI), which operate courses and diving trips. The dives near the jetties are shallow, about 8m (26ft),

Goa has diving opportunities for all, beginners and experienced divers alike

The luxurious swimming pool at the Marriott

with variable visibility. Some of the sites are off islands, reached after a 15- to 30-minute boat ride. The schools list dive sites for beginners, in sheltered coves and near jetties, but those with strong currents are only suitable for experienced divers. A variety of fish can be seen, as well as crustaceans, morays, hard corals and sea fans, and some of the dive sites include wrecks that are colonised by marine wildlife. Diving trips are also operated to Devbagh Island and other sites in Karnataka near the Goan border.

Barracuda Diving India. Sun Village Resort, Baga. Tel: 2279409. www.barracudadiving.com

Goa Diving. 145P Chapel Bhat, Chicalim. Tel: 2555117. www.goadiving.com

Swimming pools

Almost all resorts and most of the big hotels in Goa have a swimming pool. By regulation, swimming pools at Indian hotels and resorts are shallow and prohibit diving. They have separate changing rooms, with showers, for men and women. Swimsuits are compulsory and nude swimming is not allowed. Towels are provided and many hotels have smaller pools for children, as well as whirlpools next to the main pool. Pools are cleaned regularly and it is a good idea to follow specified swimming-pool opening times to avoid chemicals and soaps. Some hotel pools permit non-residents, for an admission charge.

Swimming pools at clubs and sports complexes usually follow international competitive standards regarding size and depth, and many have diving boards.

Tennis, badminton and squash

Most of the bigger resorts and hotels, and almost all clubs, have facilities for these popular games.

Volleyball

Volleyball is popular at school and college level and you will see volleyball courts at many villages. Some of the beaches also have volleyball courts for visitors.

HEALTH CLUBS, SPAS AND YOGA

Health clubs

Many hotels and resorts have health clubs with a gym, sauna and steam bath. Use of the gym is usually free for hotel residents. Most health clubs are managed by a team of supervisors responsible for maintaining the equipment and assisting guests. A few hotels and resorts also have daily aerobics sessions and weight-training instructors. The health clubs generally have separate sections for men and women, but some may also have different timings.

Long-staying visitors to Goa can also become members of health clubs with qualified instructors. Inspect the equipment and hygiene standards before joining a programme.

Spas

Ayurveda is enormously popular in Goa, and many resorts and hotels have Ayurvedic centres offering massages, treatments, short programmes and packages customised for specific ailments. Most of them have a qualified physician who prescribes the treatment and diet, separate rooms for men and women, and steam baths. Ayurvedic massage and treatment centres have also opened on popular beaches. Government-certified Ayurvedic centres must meet certain minimum standards, but it is a good idea to verify a facility's credentials and hygiene standards before enrolling.

Besides Ayurvedic massage and therapy, a number of upmarket resorts in Goa offer Southeast Asian aromatherapy, Thai and Balinese massage, Swedish massage, hydrotherapy and other spa treatments.

Massages

Masseurs peddle their services at many of the beaches, and hotel health clubs may also have a massage room. Ayurvedic massage centres have opened at some of the tourist centres, with strict guidelines laid down by the state government.

Yoga and meditation

With the increasing international interest in these ancient Asian disciplines for physical and spiritual well-being, several hotels and resorts have made yoga, meditation and Ayurvedic therapies available to their guests. Both short- and long-term courses are offered, and at some upmarket resorts there are daily sessions for beginners at fixed hours.

For more serious yoga students, the beginner and advanced courses at ashrams and government-approved institutions may be preferable. The Kaivalyadhama Yoga Institute at Lonavala (*tel: (02114) 273039. www.kdham.com*) is one of the best known in India.

Yoga is also a regular feature of Goa's beaches, where you will see lots of flyers and boards advertising yoga classes. Some world-class yoga teachers also come to Goa in season to teach at beaches such as Anjuna, Arambol, Vagator, Benaulim and Palolem.

WALKING

Goa offers plenty of variety for those who love walking. There are narrow roads through the old quarters of cities and towns, village paths that offer a glimpse of rural India, coastal roads through palm groves, winding paths in the hills and in plantation areas, and strenuous treks in the Western Ghats.

BIRDWATCHING

Birdwatching in Goa is very rewarding. Your hotel should be able to refer you to specialist tour operators or guides that take birdwatching trips or guided nature walks. Visitors to Goa will return with a healthy checklist of birds seen – and even more heard, because spotting is difficult in the Western Ghats – at the various sites in the state.

Besides the wildlife reserves of Goa (*see pp64–5*), birdwatching guides take visitors to the forests of Tambdi Surla, where Malabar hornbill, frogmouth, blue-eared kingfisher, Indian pitta, Malabar trogon, Scops owl, eagle owl and woodpeckers are among the key species. The coastal areas of Morjim are good for shorebirds, while Cabo De Rama is renowned for its sea eagles, and Carambolim and Mayem lakes for waterfowl.

Yoga on the beach, Cavelossim

Food and drink

Visitors will find a delightful variety of food in Goa. Goan seafood features prominently on the menu of restaurants clustered along the coast, but you will also find lamb, mutton (goat), beef, pork, chicken and duck, and a variety of fresh vegetables, cooked in the locally grown spices. Foodies will enjoy the fusion of South Indian and Portuguese gastronomic influences.

Besides promoting regional Goan cuisine, Goa's tourism boom ensures that dishes of other regions such as North India, Gujarat and South India are easily available. International cuisine is common as well; chefs from overseas often spend the winter in Goa catering to international visitors.

Where to eat

Remember that Indian food can be a lot more spicy on its home ground than at curry restaurants abroad. Hotels, resorts and restaurants in the tourist centres are accustomed to travellers and prepare food to suit the foreign palate.

At five-star hotels you will find a wide choice of cuisine, from French and Italian to Thai, Mughlai and South Indian, as well as lavish buffets.

Beach cafés and restaurants are usually temporary shacks or kiosks that operate during the holiday season. They are popular places for juices, fizzy drinks, beer and other alcoholic drinks, tea, coffee and snacks on the beach. A variety of local curries is served there, but they also have western menu options.

The menu revolves around what is available. Many shacks have an electricity supply for refrigeration but it is still best to eat only what you know is fresh.

Street-side eating places, called *dhabas*, are also relatively safe, as the turnover is high and the menu is limited to a few simple items. Because they cater to the local population, the food is more authentic than that served in the tourist centres and hotels (it is also spicier).

Health issues

One of India's greatest health hazards for visitors is its drinking water. Drinking straight from a tap, or using tap water for cleaning teeth, is an open invitation to water-borne diseases, as the public water supply is often contaminated. Bottled water is widely available, but check the seal properly and crush the bottle before disposing of it so that it can't be refilled. Decent restaurants should open the sealed bottle in front of you to alleviate any concerns. If you are visiting someone's home, ask if the water is 'purified'. Carry water sterilisation tablets and a filter just in case bottled water is not available.

Fruits, vegetables, cold meats and fish, which have been exposed to flies or washed in dirty water, as well as undercooked meats and vegetables, are risky even in big hotels. Shellfish is not recommended unless you know that it is very fresh.

Drinks

Tea, or *chai*, is made in Indian homes and restaurants by brewing tea leaves, milk, water and sugar. This is usually a safe drink to have, and it is often easily available at street-side kiosks, railway stations and on trains. *Masala chai* includes powdered spices such as ginger, cardamom or cinnamon. In tourist resorts tea is more likely to be served with milk and sugar separate.

Likewise, coffee is served white, brewed with milk and sugar unless specified in homes and local restaurants, while more foreign-oriented establishments will adapt to meet tourists' preferences. Espresso and cappuccino are becoming popular, and South India is famous for its local-style filter coffee.

Another popular beverage in India is *lassi* or *chaas*, which is buttermilk made by churning yoghurt. It contains water,

so be wary if you're in a downmarket establishment. Similarly, make sure that fruit juices are served without water or ice.

A local Goan drink is *feni*. *Kaju feni* is the fermented juice of the cashew apple, while *coconut feni* or *palm feni* is the fermented sap of the coconut palm. You can try it with soda or in a fruit cocktail.

Fruit

Goa grows a variety of fruits, and is particularly known for its alphonso mango. Papaya, pineapple, guava, jackfruit, oranges and sweet lime are also grown locally, and other fruits like apple and pear are available, too. Peel the fruit before eating, or at least wash it in purified water.

Breakfast

At hotels, breakfast is usually a lavish buffet. Even at smaller hotels, packaged cereals with milk, fried eggs or omelette and buttered toast are the usual breakfast options, with North or South Indian breakfast items also available.

If you are eating out at street-side restaurants, the usual breakfast options are *puri* (deep-fried whole-wheat rounds) with vegetables, *parathas* (Indian whole-wheat bread cooked and usually stuffed with potatoes and other vegetables), *idlis* (rice dumplings), *wadas* (deep-fried savoury doughnuts) or *dosas* (savoury rice pancakes, usually stuffed with potatoes, and served with a lentil soup, *sambar*, and a coconut chutney).

Indian food

When a restaurant gives you an Indian menu it usually lists North Indian preparations. This is also called Punjabi or Mughlai cuisine. North Indian meals are rich, with liberal use of cream and nuts.

South Indian restaurants serve pure vegetarian food, although most restaurants that see foreign trade have some meat options on the menu. Rice is the mainstay of the diet and is served with curries containing coconut or tamarind. Snacks such as *dosas*, *wadas* and *idlis* are extremely popular.

Meal or *thali*

A 'meal' or a *thali* refers to a simple set menu with a fixed price served to everyone. It is usually good, quick, reasonably priced and freshly prepared.

A vegetarian meal usually includes vegetables, chapatti, pulses, rice, pickles, yoghurts and sauces, and occasionally a local sweet served on a metal platter, with the individual items in little bowls.

Non-vegetarian meals include mutton, chicken or fish dishes.

Ice cream

Well-known Indian brands are Vadilal and Amul plus international names such as Walls and Baskins-Robbins. Amul also offers Indian ice cream called *kulfis*. Avoid ice cream from hawkers.

Eating out price guide

The following categories are based on the price of an average meal per person, excluding drinks:

★ Less than Rs 200
★★ Rs 200–500
★★★ Rs 500–1,000
★★★★ above Rs 1,000

Most of the restaurants in Goa's tourist resorts operate from October to April, while urban eateries are more likely to be open year-round.

CENTRAL GOA
Panaji
Kamat ★
South Indian vegetarian fare is the thing at this simple, central eatery. Meals are served thali-style, and you can also enjoy sweets, ice cream and milkshakes.
5 Church Square, Panaji. Tel: 2426116.
Open: daily 8am–9.30pm.

Quarterdeck ★★
This hotel-restaurant enjoys an excellent location, with its large terrace overlooking the river adorned with fairy lights. Quarterdeck is a multi-cuisine eatery, with Indian, Chinese and vegetarian options predominant.
Opp. Hotel Mandovi, DB Marg,
Panaji. Tel: 2432905.
Email: mandovi_goa@sancharnet.in.
www.hotelmandovigoa.com.
Open: daily 11am–11pm.

Sher-e-Punjab ★★
Bright and clean family eatery doing tandoori and Punjabi cuisine. The

portions are filling and the service attentive.
Rua 18th June, Panaji.
Tel: 2227204.
Email: butterchicken@
sher-e-punjab.com.
www.sher-e-punjab.com.
Open: daily 11.30am–3pm
& 6.30–10pm.

Viva Panjim ★★
Increasingly popular with tourists, and therefore sometimes fairly busy, this attractively lit and decorated courtyard restaurant serves up Goan and Indian favourites. Sit outside or in the air-conditioned interior section.
178 Rua 31 de Janeiro,
Fontainhas, Panaji.
Tel: 2422405,
9850471363. Open: daily
11.30am–3pm & 7–11pm.

Panjim Inn Restaurant
★★–★★★
This laid-back eatery is as stylish and elegant as the well-known heritage hotel of which it is part. If things are quiet, diners can pop into the kitchen, which rustles up local and continental cuisine, and get involved. The first-floor veranda is a great spot for watching the world go by.

31st January Road,
Panaji. Tel: 2226523.
www.panjiminn.com.
Open: daily 11am–11pm.

Barbecue ★★★
The large, open grill, allowing you to select your food, specify the cooking instructions and then watch it being prepared by the accommodating and friendly staff, is the big attraction at this large, beachside restaurant.
Cidade de Goa,
Vainguinim Beach,
Dona Paula, Panaji.
Tel: 2454545.
www.cidadedegoa.com.
Open: daily 7.30–11pm.

Horseshoe ★★★
Enjoy Goan and Portuguese cuisine – fish curry and spicy chicken are two of the highlights – in intimate surroundings.
E245 Rua de Ourem,
Panaji. Tel: 2431788.
Open: daily 7–10.30pm.

Simply Fish ★★★★
This seasonal piscatorial restaurant is one of the Marriott's slew of top-class eateries. The seafood is cooked to each diner's specifications, and the atmosphere –

with tables overlooking the water – is perfect.
Marriott, Miramar,
Panaji. Tel: 2463333.
www.marriott.com.
Open: Nov–Apr daily
7–11pm.

Ponda
Café Bhonsle ★
Popular, centrally located veggie eatery that serves up cheap eats to Ponda people. There's not much in the way of frills, but if you want fast, decent food in clean surroundings, you're in the right place.
Royal Apartment,
Kaziwada Road, opp.
Saraswat Cooperative
Bank, Ponda.
Tel: 2318725. Open:
Mon–Sat 7am–10pm, Sun
7am–3pm.

SOUTHERN GOA
Benaulim
Pedro's ★–★★
Bright and cheerful Pedro's has now been operating for over 40 years. The live music, western and Goan, is a highlight of this venerable beach shack, which also has a small dance floor.

At intersection of beach and road, Benaulim. Tel: 9822389177. Open: daily 8.30–1.30am.

Roger's Hygienic Kitchen ★★

Choose some reading material from the charity bookshop, knock some pool balls around or digest your dinner on a comfortable chair at this beachside eatery, which has a hint of North Africa about the décor. *To the right of the car park, Benaulim. Tel: 9822488079. Open: daily 6am–last customer (around 1–3am).*

Cavelossim

Riverside ★★★★

Top-class Italian cuisine, a mesmerising waterside location and impeccable service make the Riverside in hotel Leela Kempinski one of the best places to eat in the area. The Leela has several other excellent eateries, including opulent signature restaurant Jamavar, for Goan and Indian fine dining. *Leela Kempinski, Mobor, Cavelossim. Tel: 6621234. www.theleela.com. Open: daily 7.30–10.30pm.*

Margao

Banjara ★

Candlelit and cosy, Banjara's North Indian cuisine is the most popular of its offerings, and there's also a children's menu. Service is prompt and professional. *Desouza Chambers, near Grace Church, New Market, Margao. Tel: 2722008. Open: daily 11am–3pm & 7pm–midnight.*

NORTHERN GOA

Baga

Nilaya Hermitage ★★★

Poolside dining at a well-known boutique hotel. European and Indian food both feature on the set menus. *Arpora Bhati, Baga. Tel: 2276793. www.nilaya.com. Open: daily 8am–10pm.*

Calangute

La Fenice & Coffee Garden ★★

The imported ingredients, authentic coffee and freshly made pasta all contribute to this Italian eatery's ongoing popularity. Opt

for a table on the rooftop terrace – the restaurant is on three levels. Pastas, meat dishes and dreamy desserts all win enthusiastic plaudits. *Candolim-Calangute Road, Gaura Vaddo opposite the old Ice Factory. Tel: 0832 2281182. www.abcfarmsindia.com. Open: Mon–Sun 10.30am–midnight.*

Souza Lobo ★★

This long-standing, family-run restaurant, now nearly 80 years old, serves up Goan, tandoori, Chinese and continental dishes, which can be washed down with homemade *feni*. The seafood and salads are particularly good. There's a relaxed atmosphere, regular live music and an excellent seafront location. *On the beach, central Calangute. Tel: 2281234. Email: jude@souzalobo.com. www.souzalobo.com. Open: daily 11am–11pm.*

Tibetan Kitchen ★★

Western food joins the Tibetan fare at this highly reputed place, now going for 20 years, where the vibe is

laid-back and the portions generous. When your appetite is sated, you can pass the time playing a board game or perusing a magazine.
Set back in an alleyway off Beach Road, close to the beach, Calangute. Tel: 2275744, 9326137750. Email: thetibkit@yahoo.com. Open: daily 9am–2pm & 5pm–midnight.

After Seven ★★★
Chefs schooled in top international hotel chains rustle up superlative European cuisine in a glass-fronted kitchen at this popular eatery in the grounds of the owner's house.
1/274B Chapel Lane, Gaura Vaddo, off main Calangute–Candolim road, Calangute. Tel: 2279757, 9226188288. Email: aftersevenrestaurant@ yahoo.com. www. aftersevenrestaurant.com. Open: daily 7–11.30pm.

Sinquerim
The Stone House ★★
Set in the eponymous house and its verdant courtyard, this renowned

long-timer serves up highly reputed Indian, Goan and Portuguese food, often with liberal use of spices. Fairy lights bedeck the exterior and there is usually live jazz, blues or other soothing strains to dine to.
Fort Aguada Road. Tel: 247 9909. Open: Mon–Sun 6pm–midnight.

Banyan Tree ★★★★
Sophisticated dining beneath the eponymous 300-plus-year-old tree. Service is exemplary and a new Thai chef joins the staff every year, to keep the fabulous food – of which the green curry is a highlight – fresh and exciting.
Taj Holiday Village, Sinquerim. Tel: 664 5858. Open: Sept–May daily 12.30–2.45pm & 7.30–10.30pm, Jun–Aug daily 7.30–10.30pm.

OUTSIDE GOA
Mumbai
Bade Miya ★
Legendary street-stall offering cheap, spicy eats. The kebabs and rolls are the mainstays, but there are a few Indian staples for vegetarians. A

gastronomic experience that is quintessential Mumbai.
Tullock Rd, Apollo Bandar, Colaba. Tel: (022) 22848038. Open: daily 7am–1am.

The Great Wall ★★★★
Chefs flown in from China ensure that the exquisite cuisine is authentic. Close to the airport, this Leela hotel and its dining options are a great choice if you have a long layover.
Leela Kempinski, Sahar Mumbai. Tel: (022) 66911234. Open: daily 12.30–2.45pm & 7–11.30pm.

India Jones ★★★★
Based on the travels of Bharat Joyent (aka India Jones), this classy restaurant serves up sumptuous cuisine from seven Asian countries. An open kitchen, into which diners are welcome to wander, adds to the charm. The Trident's other flagship eatery is Mediterranean restaurant Frangipani.
Trident Hotel, Nariman Point. Tel: (022) 66324343. Open: daily 12.30–2.45pm & 7.30–11.45pm.

Goan cuisine

Goan food has similarities with other Indian food, but makes use of locally grown ingredients such as coconuts, cashews, spices, chillies and kokum, made from a fruit. Most of the dishes are flavoured with coconut milk, coconut oil, grated coconut flesh or toddy, the sap from the coconut palm. Goans also use jaggery, brown sugar drawn from the date palm, for making sweets. Spices, such as cumin, coriander, chilli, garlic and turmeric, are used to give the strong taste and aroma that typify Goan cooking.

A coastal state, Goa also depends on the harvest of the sea: lobster, crab, crayfish, prawns, shrimps, squid and a variety of fish including snappers, pomfret, mackerel, sardines, kingfish and shark. Fish curry and rice is a Goan staple. Goans also eat pork (except for the small Muslim community), mutton, lamb and chicken, and beef is commonly eaten by the Christians of Goa.

Some well-known Goan preparations are *ambottik*, a sour hot curry for fish but occasionally also for other seafood and meats; *caldeirada* or *caldeen*, a mild seafood dish with or without wine; and *recheido*, fish stuffed with spicy red curry. *Cafrial* is usually a dry, fried chicken marinated in chillies, garlic and ginger, and *xacuti* is a pungent curry with coconut milk usually meant for cooking chicken. *Balchao* is a method of cooking lobster, prawn or fish in a chilli-red, tangy curry. Two of Goa's most famous dishes are *Vindaloo*, pork or fish in vinegar, and *Sorpotel*, diced pork, liver and heart in a spicy thick sauce usually flavoured with *feni* (a strong spirit). Because of the preservative quality of the *Balchao*, *Vindaloo* and *Sorpotel* curries, prawns, fish and meat in these sauces are available bottled or packed. As

Fish drying on Colva Beach

Fresh food markets are laden with produce

the names suggest, the Portuguese influence on Goa's culture is evident in the cuisine.

Goan sausages are available in the markets and are made from salted and spicy pieces of pork. Vegetarian dishes include pumpkin, breadfruit and papaya curries. Starters are usually shrimps baked in pies or rice pastry shells, while steamed crab and lobsters are served whole.

Condiments include *kishmur* (crushed dry shrimp), often scattered over the main course. The curries are commonly served with short-grained red, brown or white rice.

The Portuguese introduced bread to Goa, and bakers or their delivery staff regularly do the rounds on bicycles, delivering breads in the morning. The *pao* is the typical crusty bread of Goa.

Another kind of local bread is *sana* – steamed rice rolls flavoured with coconut and toddy. These breads are ideal for soaking up the gravies.

The typical sweet of Goa is *bebinca*, a layered coconut and jaggery pancake made using eggs and sugar. *Batica* is a coconut cake usually served with ice cream. *Dodol* is painstakingly made during feasts and holidays using fresh coconut milk, jaggery and coconuts cooled in a flat pan and served sliced.

While authentic Goan cooking is available in a few hotels, resorts and restaurants, the beach shacks have evolved their own styles of cooking for the tastes of Western tourists, such as fried, grilled and steamed seafood in butter and garlic sauce.

Accommodation

Goa has a huge variety of accommodation, ranging from family-run guesthouses to upmarket resorts. Visitors can expect to find a hotel that suits their needs and their budget in most places. However, hotels in India suffer from a number of problems that visitors may not have experienced elsewhere, such as dust, mosquitoes and other insects, power cuts and water shortages.

Price categories

Hotels are graded from one-star to five-star deluxe, with categories of four-star and above given by the central government authorities and the lower star classifications by the state government. Hotels are judged on a number of predetermined standards, from ambience and room size to the qualifications of the staff, services and facilities.

Five-star deluxe hotels have extensive facilities, including modern rooms, round-the-clock room service, swimming pools, bar, 24-hour coffee shop and restaurants. Five-star and four-star hotels are a cut below the five-star deluxe hotels, while three-star hotels maintain reasonably good standards without the frills of a five-star.

Budget stays

India has many modestly priced hotels. Most of them are located near railway stations, bus stations or near the market, and standards vary considerably. Some can be great value for money, while others are downright dirty.

Before booking into a really low-priced hotel, it is important to inspect the rooms to check the standards of cleanliness and to ensure that everything works.

Forest lodges

The forest department has lodges and resthouses inside most Indian wildlife reserves. Like the other government guesthouses, these are beautifully located but are rarely well managed and can be difficult to book prior to arrival.

Privately owned lodges, resorts and camps are generally located near the entrance to or in peripheral areas of the reserves. These are available for visitors to the wildlife reserves.

Government guesthouses

Government guesthouses, such as the Circuit Houses in cities, and the Public

Hotel in Panaji

Accommodation at Tiracol Fort

Works Department Resthouses, which are located outside the cities and towns, are often grand colonial buildings with equally impressive rooms. Most of them have highly desirable locations, but unfortunately many of them are poorly managed and maintained. Moreover, rooms are generally reserved for government officials, so finding accommodation can be difficult.

Heritage hotels

Buildings built before 1935 that have been opened for visitors are called heritage hotels in India. These buildings have to be sympathetically restored and renovated with their historic value in mind to qualify as a heritage hotel. This is not a homogeneous concept, and it covers a variety of types of accommodation, from five-star deluxe palace hotels to family-owned ancestral houses.

Goa has just a few heritage hotels, such as Tiracol Fort (*www.forttiracol.com*), Siolim House (*www.siolimhouse.com*), Panjim Inn and Panjim Pousada (*www.panjiminn.com*). The idea of reusing heritage properties for financial benefit is appealing to many owners in Goa who are finding it expensive to maintain stately houses. Besides Goa, Pune and Kolhapur also have heritage hotels.

Plantation houses

In India, it is possible to stay at farmhouses and plantation bungalows as guests of the plantation owners, from the tea estates of Assam and Darjeeling in northeastern India to the tea, coffee and spice plantations of Kerala and Karnataka in southwestern India. The experience includes touring the plantations to see the cultivation, harvesting and processing activities, learning about the medicinal uses of the plants, walking nature trails to spot birds and butterflies, visiting nearby villages for an insight into local culture, tasting the produce, sampling food made from locally grown fruits, vegetables and spices, getting access to planters' clubs and sports facilities, and often interacting with the families who own the plantations. In Goa, plantations that offer accommodation include Rustic Plantations (*tel: (0832) 2379191*), which is one of the few places to stay in the Bicholim and Satari hills, and Savoi Plantation (*www.savoiplantation.com*) with mud houses facing the crops.

Railway retiring rooms

Most railway stations have private rooms and dormitories that are handy for travellers. These are in high demand and are almost always full.

Tents and camps

The standard of campsites is very variable, and it is important to check the quality before booking. 'Swiss tents' generally refer to high-quality, spacious tents with private baths and a sitting area in front. They are usually set on plinths and are quite comfortable. 'Rajasthani tents' or 'royal tents' are becoming extremely popular at beach resorts in Goa. Based on the design of the royal hunting camps of the Maharajas and Nawabs of Rajasthan, Gujarat and Central India, these tents are generally large with attractive tie-dyed, embroidered or appliquéd fabrics as the inner lining, antique-style furniture and bathrooms with showers and western fittings. Many of these tents pop up during the winter season as 'temporary resort accommodation' on beaches where there are building restrictions. Deluxe or luxury tented resorts, semi-permanent structures with canopies over them to look like tents, have also been erected at beaches, and they can be as good as hotels.

Nature camps are generally on the simple side, and facilities can even be very basic in some of them. Many of these camps have been set up as permanent or semi-permanent nature resorts in forested areas such as Tambdi Surla near the Karnataka border. The prices at these nature camps may include activities such as birdwatching, butterfly spotting, elephant rides, yoga and village walks. Hiking and camping in two-person tents are offered by some tour operators and youth organisations.

Tourist bungalows

Tourism development corporations are public-sector companies that own and manage hotels called tourist bungalows in most states of India. They can be good-value options for travellers, but standards vary considerably, and as they are government managed the service is not always comparable to that in privately owned properties. Goa Tourism Development Corporation (GTDC, *www.goa-tourism.com*) has tourist bungalows at destinations such as Panaji, Miramar near Panaji, Old Goa, Farmagudi near Ponda, Calangute, Mapusa, Britona, Margao, Vasco and Colva.

Upmarket resorts

Resorts at the beaches or hill stations have a special attraction because of their location. Goa has some of India's most famous beach resorts, especially in Salcette Taluka. Sprawling complexes, they provide idyllic settings for those who want to indulge in the vast range of facilities available. Such resorts are heavily booked in the winter months from October to March, so early advance reservations are recommended.

Miramar Residency boutique hotel, Panaji

Accommodation price guide

Prices are based on a double room per night for two people, with breakfast, in high season. Many Goan hotels shut for the monsoon season. Those that stay open often charge significantly lower rates during this period.

★ under Rs 1,000
★★ Rs 1,000–2,500
★★★ Rs 2,500–4,000
★★★★ over Rs 4,000

CENTRAL GOA
Panaji
Panjim Inn ★★–★★★★

It's the old-school charm and hospitality that have made the trio of Panjim heritage properties – Inn, Peoples and Pousada – such a consistent hit with visitors. Situated close together in the heart of the Latin quarter, Peoples offers wonderfully elegant rooms with four-poster beds and mosaic-tile bathrooms, with Inn and Pousada lower-cost takes on the same atmosphere and style.

*31st January Road, Panaji.
Tel: 2226523. Email:
panjiminn@bsnl.in.
www.panjiminn.com*

Devaaya ★★★

With a serene location on Divar Island, this unusual resort offers a raft of ayurvedic and natural therapies, as well as yoga, to relax and revive you. The stylish accommodation and inviting pool add to the atmosphere. Treatment packages require a minimum seven-night stay.

*Divar Island, Panaji.
Tel: 2280500. Email:
info@devaaya.com.
www.devaaya.com*

Cidade de Goa ★★★★

The huge, attractive rooms are among the highlights at this sunny Portuguese-themed beach resort. There is plenty to do here and lots of pleasant spots to take a seat and enjoy the surroundings.

*Vainguinim Beach,
Dona Paula, Panaji.
Tel: 2454545. Email:
sales@cidadedegoa.com.
www.cidadedegoa.com*

Marriott ★★★★

The reliably splendid Marriott has recently undergone renovation.
Style, taste and luxury infuse every part of this Miramar hotel, from the elegant rooms to the delectable cuisine.

*Miramar Beach.
Tel: 2463333.
www.marriott.com*

Ponda
Hotel Sungrace ★

Sitting atop a bustling local restaurant, this centrally located hotel is popular with Indian guests, so it can be worth phoning ahead. The clean, up-to-date rooms come either with or without air conditioning.

*Near the bus stand,
Ponda. Tel: 2311238.*

SOUTHERN GOA
Cavelossim
Dona Sylvia ★★★★

Spread out over 26 acres, this spacious, verdant resort offers comfortable, roomy accommodation a short walk from the beach, either American plan or all inclusive. Designed in a Mediterranean style, rooms have a terrace or veranda. The resort offers a plethora of activities and family entertainment, from a surfeit of sports to a kids' club to a spa.

Cavelossim, Mobor. Tel: 2871888. Email: info@donasylvia.com. www.donasylvia.com

Leela Kempinski ★★★★

Luxury doesn't get much more absolute than at the Leela chain's Goan outfit. Boasting classy, sumptuous rooms with lagoon views, a selection of top eateries and even its own golf course, there's service and style in abundance.

Cavelossim, Mobor. Tel: 6621234. Email: reservations.goa@theleela. com. www.theleela.com

Palolem

Palolem Guest House ★

Rather more substantial than much of Palolem's beach shack accommodation, rooms at this bright and cheery guesthouse have the option of air conditioning and balcony.

South of the beach, Ourem, Palolem. Tel: 2644879. Email: palolemguesthouse@ hotmail.com. www. palolemguesthouse.com

NORTHERN GOA

Anjuna

Palacete Rodrigues ★★

Housed in a Portuguese mansion with old-school furniture, Palacete Rodrigues' selling point is elegance on a budget. The 15 rooms have optional air conditioning, and the famous market and beach are not far away.

Mazal Vaddo, Anjuna. Tel: 2273358. Email: info@palacetegoa.com. www.palacetegoa.com

Calangute

Coco Banana ★-★★

In premises that date from the 1920s, this amiable Goan-Swiss family-run place consists of simple rooms with two larger apartments nearby. Spick and span facilities and a tranquil location are among the things that recommend this bargain option.

Off the beach, south of main road, Calangute. Tel: 2279068. Email: cocobanana@ rediffmail.com. www.cocobananagoa.com

Candolim

Victor Exotica ★★★

Set around the swimming pool, three-star Victor Exotica is centrally located with a fun family atmosphere. Live evening entertainment adds to the jolly vibe.

Candolim. Tel: 2479515. Email: reservations@ alconvictorgroup.com. www.victorexoticagoa.com

OUTSIDE GOA

Mumbai (Bombay)

Columbus ★★★

Helpful staff and a quiet location make this northern hotel a good mid-range choice. Effort has gone into making the rooms modern, clean and comfortable. Airport pick-up is included.

344, Nanda Patkar Road, Vile Parle. Tel: (22) 42144343. Email: info@hotelcolumbus.in. www.hotelcolumbus.in

Leela Kempinski ★★★★

Its proximity to both airports makes the Leela ideal for an indulgent stopover en route to or from Goa. There's luxury and comfort in spades, a fabulous pool area and the service is exemplary.

Sahar Mumbai.
Tel: (22) 66911234. Email:
reservations.mumbai@
theleela.com
www.theleela.com

Trident ★★★★
Plush and stylish, the
Trident oozes five-star
class, with spacious
rooms and a chic design.

Nariman Point.
Tel: (22) 66324343.
Email: reservations@
tridenthotels.com.
www.tridenthotels.com

The Taj Exotica resort, Southern Goa

Practical guide

Arriving
International
At the time of writing there are still no scheduled direct international flights to Goa's Dabolim Airport from Europe, although India's Central Civil Aviation Ministry was planning to permit them in the future. Almost all visitors who do not arrive on charter flights take an international flight to Mumbai (*see pp106–16*) and then a domestic flight or train to Goa.

Domestic
Domestic airlines, such as Indian Airlines, Jet Airways, JetLite, Spicejet, Kingfisher Airlines, Go Air, IndiGo, and Paramount Airways, connect Goa to Mumbai and other international airport cities such as Delhi, Chennai, Ahmedabad, Bangalore and Kolkata. The overnight train from Mumbai to Margao in Goa is a convenient and economical option.

Airports and customs
Visitors are allowed to bring into the country personal items, wines and other alcoholic drinks up to a maximum of 1 litre, 50 cigars, 200 cigarettes or 250g of tobacco, and duty-free gifts up to a maximum value of Rs 5,000.

Any expensive personal effects or equipment like binoculars and cameras should be registered for re-export. Keep registration numbers handy, especially for laptops, cameras and other expensive equipment, as these are required when you fill in the re-export form. There is a departure tax for international flights, but most airlines add it to their fare.

Airline websites
Air India *www.airindia.com*
Go Air *www.goair.in*
Indian Airlines
www.indian-airlines.nic.in
IndiGo *www.goindigo.in*
Jet Airways *www.jetairways.com*
JetLite *www.jetlite.com*
Kingfisher Airlines
www.flykingfisher.com
Paramount Airways
www.paramountairways.com
Spicejet *www.spicejet.com*

Crossing the river in Goa

Goan car number plate adorned for good luck

Documentation

Travellers from most countries (except Nepal and Bhutan) need a valid passport, which must expire no earlier than six months after your intended departure date, and visa. You should also carry a set of photocopies in case you lose the originals.

Climate

Goa has a more or less equitable climate all year round, rarely rising above 35°C (95°F) and seldom dropping below 18°C (64°F), but in the hills it can get cooler in the peak tourist season from November to April. The four months of rainfall from July to September are preceded by two months of humidity.

The monsoon

The southwest monsoon blows in from the Arabian Sea and is condensed by the cooler climes of the Western Ghats, causing torrential rains, lashing waves and powerful winds. There is another wet

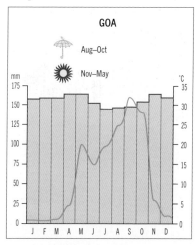

WEATHER CONVERSION CHART

25.4mm = 1 inch

$°F = 1.8 × °C + 32$

spell in November and December, which is caused by the retreating monsoon from the eastern Bay of Bengal.

Clothing

Loose-fitting light cottons are most suited to the warm and humid weather of Goa, but it is a good idea to carry a jacket or a sweater for the evenings, especially if destinations in the Western Ghats, such as the hill stations of Mahableshwan and Lonavala, are part of your itinerary. Long-sleeved clothes in light colours provide some protection from mosquitoes.

As a tourist, informal clothes are generally acceptable, but bring some more formal clothes for big hotels, smart restaurants and parties. Wear comfortable shoes and sandals that allow your feet to breathe. Laundry is inexpensive and rarely takes more than 24 hours, but delicate clothes should be washed personally.

Communications

India is a computer-oriented society, and Goa has plenty of places where you can get online. Most travellers find the poste restante and speedpost services reliable, but the regular postal services are inconsistent.

There are courier services in big cities that guarantee 'desk to desk' delivery, while a local courier service, called *angadia*, operates to smaller towns and villages.

Currency

The Indian currency is the rupee, which is divided into units of 100 *paise*. Notes are printed in denominations

A hot day's labour on the beach at Anjuna

of Rs 1,000, 500, 100, 50, 20, 10 and 5 while coins are minted in Rs 10, 5, 2, 1, 0.50, 0.25, 0.20, 0.10 and 0.05. Keep small notes handy, as it is difficult to get change on small purchases.

Currency exchange

It is not possible to order rupees in your home country, so you will need to change currency on arrival. Money exchange is not a problem as banks, hotels and licensed private moneychangers or authorised dealers will happily change dollars or sterling for rupees. Collect your encashment certificate, which you will need to reconvert currency. The certificates also help you to pay in rupees at tourist quota counters at railway stations.

Traveller's cheques

Thomas Cook's traveller's cheques are widely accepted for exchange and as payment at hotels, and they are a relatively safe way of carrying money.

Credit cards

Almost all star-category hotels and resorts, expensive restaurants and established shops accept Visa and MasterCard.

Tipping

It is customary to tip 10 per cent at restaurants, Rs 10 to Rs 20 each to hotel porters, and Rs 50 to Rs 100 a day to drivers. Hotel staff will also expect a tip.

CONVERSION TABLE

FROM	TO	MULTIPLY BY
Inches	Centimetres	2.54
Feet	Metres	0.3048
Yards	Metres	0.9144
Miles	Kilometres	1.6090
Acres	Hectares	0.4047
Gallons	Litres	4.5460
Ounces	Grams	28.35
Pounds	Grams	453.6
Pounds	Kilograms	0.4536
Tons	Tonnes	1.0160

To convert back, for example from centimetres to inches, divide by the number in the third column.

MEN'S SUITS

UK	36	38	40	42	44	46	48
Rest of Europe	46	48	50	52	54	56	58
USA	36	38	40	42	44	46	48

DRESS SIZES

UK	8	10	12	14	16	18
France	36	38	40	42	44	46
Italy	38	40	42	44	46	48
Rest of Europe	34	36	38	40	42	44
USA	6	8	10	12	14	16

MEN'S SHIRTS

UK	14	14.5	15	15.5	16	16.5	17
Rest of Europe	36	37	38	39/40	41	42	43
USA	14	14.5	15	15.5	16	16.5	17

MEN'S SHOES

UK	7	7.5	8.5	9.5	10.5	11
Rest of Europe	41	42	43	44	45	46
USA	8	8.5	9.5	10.5	11.5	12

WOMEN'S SHOES

UK	4.5	5	5.5	6	6.5	7
Rest of Europe	38	38	39	39	40	41
USA	6	6.5	7	7.5	8	8.5

It is advisable to wear warmer clothing as the sun goes down

Embassies and consulates

Indian embassies abroad

Australia

3–5 Moonah Place, Yarralumla, Canberra.
Tel: (02) 6273 3999; www.hcindia-au.org

Canada

10 Springfield Road, Ottawa, K1M IC9.
Tel: (613) 744 3751; www.hciottawa.ca

New Zealand

10th floor, Princess Tower,
180 Molesworth St, Wellington.
Tel: (04) 473 6390; www.hicomind.org.nz

UK

India House, Aldwych, London
WC2B 4NA. Tel: (020) 7836 8484;
www.hcilondon.in

USA

2107 Massachusetts Avenue, NW,
Washington DC 20008.
Tel: (202) 939 7000;
www.indianembassy.org

Health

Most visitors are immunised against polio, typhoid, tetanus, and hepatitis A and B before a visit to India. For longer trips, or travellers at higher risk, Japanese B encephalitis, meningitis, TB and rabies vaccinations may be appropriate.

Take dietary precautions to prevent diarrhoea and intestinal upsets, and make sure that you slap on the sun block, as many travellers suffer sunburn and heatstroke from spending time on the beaches without adequate protection.

If you get bitten by a dog, monkey or other animal, an anti-rabies shot is essential. Ticks and leeches are common in the Western Ghats, and tick bites can cause typhus.

Hospitals and medical facilities

Generally, Goa has good doctors and there are clinics and hospitals in the cities and in most large towns. Your hotel will also be able to call a doctor for you.

Malaria

Malaria is a serious problem, so see your doctor before leaving home. Also, protect yourself against mosquito bites by covering yourself completely at night and using repellents. Malaria can be contracted even if you are taking the appropriate medication. If you have any fever or flu-like symptoms, consult a doctor.

Pharmacies

Goa has medical stores in cities, large towns and most villages. You will also find medical stores on the highways. The stores usually have local equivalents of most medicines, but carry an emergency supply of essential and prescribed medicines.

Laundry

Laundry services are inexpensive in India. Laundry shops usually do washing, ironing and dry-cleaning but can be rough with your clothes. There may be a small supplement for 'urgent' orders. Laundry services at hotels are usually much more expensive than at the shops.

Tourism office and bookshop, Panaji

Maps

Maps of Goa and neighbouring states such as Maharashtra and Karnataka are available at most bookstores. Goa Tourism also publishes maps of the state featuring tourist destinations.

Media

In Goa, you will have access to Mumbai or Bangalore editions of national English-language dailies, such as the *Times of India* and *Indian Express,* as well as locally published English dailies like *Gomantak Times, Navhind Times* and the *Herald.* News magazines such as *India Today, The Week* and *Outlook* are also available at newsstands and bookstores. A wide variety of magazines is published in India on almost every subject including business, industry and finance, cars, travel, health, cooking, sports, lifestyle and the film industry.

Almost all hotels have satellite TV in their rooms, with a choice of channels for Indian and international programmes. Besides the foreign channels, you can also access Indian news in English.

Photography

Justifiably renowned for its beautiful beaches and landscapes, Goa is extremely photogenic.

During the peak tourist season from October to March, Goa is generally sunny, except for the occasional shower in the early part of the season, and you will get plenty of colourful pictures against deep blue skies. If you need to pick up anything for your camera, such as extra memory, you'll find it in most photography shops, while enterprising street vendors also sell that sort of thing outside major tourist sites.

You will need to cushion your cameras, lenses and accessories when travelling on bumpy highways.

Post and freight

Postal services in India range from excellent to very unreliable. Send letters, postcards and parcels only from the big cities and towns and make sure the covers are franked in your presence at the counter. Important mail should be sent by registered post with a registration receipt and an attached acknowledgement card to be returned signed. Airmail and speedpost services are available at most large post offices. Stamps can be bought at the counters. Poste restante facilities are available at most post offices. Leading courier services like DHL have offices in important destinations like Panaji and Margao. It is possible to send air-freight from airports such as Dabolim, and the railways and some bus services also take domestic cargo.

Safety and security

India is a fairly safe place to travel, although Goa's reputation as a drugs market does attract undesirable elements to the state, and there have been some high-profile incidents involving tourists. Remain alert and avoid out-of-the-way places at night. The vast majority of Indians who approach you during your travels will do so out of nothing more than friendliness and curiosity; however, bear in mind that being in a foreign environment can make tourists vulnerable.

Petty thefts are not uncommon in India. A money belt is a good way to carry handy cash, and an interior pocket is good for small valuables, spare cash and photocopies of documents.

Unattended baggage is an invitation for theft; keep a padlock and chain with you to secure your baggage to any immovable object if you need to leave it for any reason.

On trains, there are wires below the bunks to which you can secure your baggage with a chain and padlock. The emergency telephone number is 108.

Sustainable tourism

Thomas Cook is a strong advocate of ethical and fairly traded tourism and believes that the travel experience should be as good for the places visited as it is for the people who visit them. That's why we firmly support The Travel Foundation, a

Practical guide

Goa is incredibly photogenic!

charity that develops solutions to help improve and protect holiday destinations, their environment, traditions and culture. To find out what you can do to make a positive difference to the places you travel to and the people who live there, please visit www.thetravelfoundation.org.uk

Telephones

India has well-developed telecommunications. There are call booths, called STD-ISD PCOs (public call offices) on all the important highways and in towns, cities and villages. These are usually cheaper than calling from hotels for national and international calls. A meter shows you how much you are spending. Many PCOs have fax machines. Fax-sending charges are based on phone rates with a supplement per page, and the PCOs will receive facsimiles on your behalf for a per page fee. There are also coin-operated phones that are an inexpensive option for calling locally. Phonecards for mobile phones called 'mobile cards', are available in India.

Time

Indian Standard Time is $5^1/_2$ hours ahead of GMT.

Toilets

Public toilets are rarely clean in India, and they are almost always of the 'hole in the ground' variety. When travelling, look for hotels and smart restaurants that are likely to have westernised cloakrooms. Keep soap and a stock of tissues handy, and, especially if travelling with children, carry a supply of antibacterial wet wipes.

Transport

See pp24–7.

Travellers with disabilities

Unfortunately, India has limited facilities for visitors with disabilities. Getting around in a wheelchair on Indian roads, which rarely have pavements, is difficult. Few hotels and monuments have ramps for wheelchair access, and bathrooms are rarely adapted for people with disabilities. Hiring a car for the tour is a possible solution, as Indian drivers are usually extremely helpful.

Voltage

Electric current is 230–240 AC, 50 cycles. Electric power cuts are frequent but usually short-lived. Bring a surge protector to protect any electrical equipment from power fluctuations. Most hotel rooms have both two-pin and three-pin sockets.

Weights and measures

India uses the metric system, where distances are in kilometres and weights in grams and kilograms. However, some imperial methods of measurement are still used in places.

Sundown over Vagator beach

Index

Acknowledgements

Thomas Cook Publishing wishes to thank the following photographers, picture libraries and other organisations, to whom the copyright belongs, for the loan of the photographs reproduced in this book:

CHAWEEWAN CHUCHUAY/CPA MEDIA 15, 23, 34, 55, 81
DREAMSTIME.COM 1 (Samrat35), 17 (Franco Cogoli), 18 (Alex Zarubin), 25, 134 (M Nekrasov), 39 (Vasile Szakacs), 108 (Aleksandar Todorovic), 121 (Attila Jandi), 123 (Shailesh Nanal), 186 (G Andrushko)
DAVID HENLEY/ CPA MEDIA 35, 36, 37, 38, 41, 46, 53, 56, 63, 65, 68, 69, 72, 73, 75, 85, 86, 87, 88, 89, 91, 93, 94, 95, 97, 99, 100, 103, 105, 109, 111, 114, 119, 127, 132, 133, 135, 136, 137, 138, 143, 151, 152, 156, 174, 177
RAINER KRACK/CPA MEDIA 11, 26, 31, 47, 44, 45, 51, 52, 59, 75, 82, 168, 169, 171, 172, 178, 179, 180, 182, 184
PICTURES COLOUR LIBRARY 21 (Clive Sawyer)
VASILE SZAKACS 13, 29, 57, 61, 80, 107, 116, 131, 144, 145, 147, 148, 153, 157, 161, 188
WIKIMEDIA COMMONS 43 (Adam Jones), 70 (Vicky)
WORLD PICTURES/PHOTOSHOT 125 (Hemis), 128 (Rick Strange), 129, 155 (Angus Gormley)

For CAMBRIDGE PUBLISHING MANAGEMENT LTD:
Project editor: Tom Lee
Typesetter: Paul Queripel
Proofreader: Catherine Burch
Indexer: Marie Lorimer

SEND YOUR THOUGHTS TO BOOKS@THOMASCOOK.COM

We're committed to providing the very best up-to-date information in our travel guides and constantly strive to make them as useful as they can be. You can help us to improve future editions by letting us have your feedback. If you've made a wonderful discovery on your travels that we don't already feature, if you'd like to inform us about recent changes to anything that we do include, or if you simply want to let us know your thoughts about this guidebook and how we can make it even better – we'd love to hear from you.

Send us ideas, discoveries and recommendations today and then look out for your valuable input in the next edition of this title.

Emails to the above address, or letters to the traveller guides Series Editor, Thomas Cook Publishing, PO Box 227, Coningsby Road, Peterborough PE3 8SB, UK.

Please don't forget to let us know which title your feedback refers to!